Web API Cookbook
Level Up Your JavaScript Applications

Joe Attardi

Beijing · Boston · Farnham · Sebastopol · Tokyo

Web API Cookbook

by Joe Attardi

Copyright © 2024 Joseph Attardi. All rights reserved.

Published by O'Reilly Media, Inc., 1005 Gravenstein Highway North, Sebastopol, CA 95472.

O'Reilly books may be purchased for educational, business, or sales promotional use. Online editions are also available for most titles (*http://oreilly.com*). For more information, contact our corporate/institutional sales department: 800-998-9938 or *corporate@oreilly.com*.

Acquisitions Editor: Amanda Quinn
Development Editor: Virginia Wilson
Production Editor: Beth Kelly
Copyeditor: Piper Editorial Consulting, LLC
Proofreader: Tove Innis

Indexer: WordCo Indexing Services, Inc.
Interior Designer: David Futato
Cover Designer: Karen Montgomery
Illustrator: Kate Dullea

April 2024:   First Edition

Revision History for the First Edition

2024-03-21:   First Release

See *http://oreilly.com/catalog/errata.csp?isbn=9781098150693* for release details.

978-1-098-15069-3

[LSI]

Table of Contents

Preface

JavaScript has come a long way since its introduction in late 1995. In the early days, the core APIs built into web browsers were limited. More advanced functionality typically required third-party JavaScript libraries, or in some cases even browser plug-ins.

A web API is a series of global objects and functions exposed by the browser. Your JavaScript code can use these to interact with the Document Object Model (DOM), perform network communication, integrate with native device features, and much more.

Polyfills

Older browsers can take advantage of some of these APIs by using polyfills. A *polyfill* is a JavaScript library that implements missing functionality. Polyfills are typically used for web API features that aren't implemented in older browsers.

While beneficial, polyfills do have some drawbacks:

- They are loaded as third-party libraries, which add to your bundle size.
- They generally aren't maintained by the browser teams, so there may be bugs or inconsistencies.
- Some advanced functionality can't be polyfilled in a performant way, or at all.

The Power of Modern Browsers

Modern web APIs have two big advantages for the web platform:

No more plug-ins
> In the past, much of this functionality was only available to native applications or clunky browser plug-ins. (Remember ActiveX and Flash?)

Fewer third-party dependencies

Modern browsers provide considerable functionality that used to require third-party JavaScript libraries. Popular libraries such as jQuery, Lodash, and Moment are usually not needed anymore.

Drawbacks of Third-Party Libraries

Third-party libraries can be helpful with older browsers or newer functionality, but they have some costs:

More code to download

Using libraries increases the amount of JavaScript the browser has to load. Whether it's bundled with your app or loaded separately from a content delivery network (CDN), your browser still has to download it. This translates into potentially longer loading times and higher battery usage on mobile devices.

Increased risk

Open source libraries, even popular ones, can be abandoned. When bugs or security vulnerabilities are found, there's no guarantee of an update. Browsers, in general, are supported by large companies (the major browsers are from Google, Mozilla, Apple, and Microsoft), and it's more likely that these issues will be fixed.

This isn't to say that third-party libraries are *bad*. There are many benefits as well, especially if you need to support older browsers. Like everything in software development, library use is a balancing act.

Who This Book Is For

This book is intended for software developers with some experience with JavaScript who want to get the most out of the web platform.

It assumes that you have a good knowledge of the JavaScript language itself: syntax, language features, and standard library functions. You should also have a working knowledge of the DOM APIs used for building interactive, browser-based JavaScript applications.

There is a wide range of recipes in this book; there's something for developers of all skill and experience levels.

What's in This Book

Each chapter contains a set of *recipes*—code examples for accomplishing a specific task. Each recipe has three sections:

Problem
> Describes the problem the recipe solves.

Solution
> Contains code and explanation that implements the recipe solution.

Discussion
> A deeper discussion of the topic. This section may contain additional code examples and comparisons with other techniques.

Code samples and live demos are on the companion website, *https://WebAPIs.info*.

Additional Resources

By its nature, the web is changing all the time. There are many great resources available online to help clarify any questions that might come up.

CanIUse.com

At the time of writing, some APIs in this book are still in development or an "experimental" phase. Watch for compatibility notes in recipes that use these APIs. For most features, you can check the latest compatibility data at *https://CanIUse.com*. You can search by the name of a feature and see the latest information about which browser versions support the API and any limitations or caveats for particular browser versions.

MDN Web Docs

MDN Web Docs (*https://oreil.ly/rLxi7*) is the de facto API documentation for all things web. It covers all the APIs from this book in great detail, as well as other topics such as CSS and HTML. It contains in-depth articles and tutorials as well as API specifications.

Specifications

When in doubt, the specification of a feature or API is the definitive resource. They aren't the most exciting reads, but they are a good place to look for details about edge cases or expected behavior.

Different APIs have different standards, but most can be found either from the Web Hypertext Application Technology Working Group (WHATWG) (*https://oreil.ly/PR0x7*) or the World Wide Web Consortium (W3C) (*https://oreil.ly/dFokl*).

The standards for ECMAScript (which specifies features in the JavaScript Language) are maintained and developed by the Ecma International Technical Committee 39, better known as TC39 (*https://tc39.es*).

Conventions Used in This Book

The following typographical conventions are used in this book:

Italic

Indicates new terms, URLs, email addresses, filenames, and file extensions.

`Constant width`

Used for program listings, as well as within paragraphs to refer to program elements such as variable or function names, databases, data types, environment variables, statements, and keywords.

`Constant width bold`

Shows commands or other text that should be typed literally by the user.

`Constant width italic`

Shows text that should be replaced with user-supplied values or by values determined by context.

 This element signifies a tip or suggestion.

 This element signifies a general note.

 This element indicates a warning or caution.

Using Code Examples

Supplemental material (code examples, exercises, etc.) is available for download at *https://github.com/joeattardi/web-api-cookbook*. Also check out the companion website (*https://WebAPIs.info*), where many of the code samples and recipes in this book are expanded into full, live, working examples.

If you have a technical question or a problem using the code examples, please send email to *bookquestions@oreilly.com*.

This book is here to help you get your job done. In general, if example code is offered with this book, you may use it in your programs and documentation. You do not need to contact us for permission unless you're reproducing a significant portion of the code. For example, writing a program that uses several chunks of code from this book does not require permission. Selling or distributing examples from O'Reilly books does require permission. Answering a question by citing this book and quoting example code does not require permission. Incorporating a significant amount of example code from this book into your product's documentation does require permission.

We appreciate, but generally do not require, attribution. An attribution usually includes the title, author, publisher, and ISBN. For example: "*Web API Cookbook* by Joseph Attardi (O'Reilly). Copyright 2024 Joe Attardi, 978-1-098-15069-3."

If you feel your use of code examples falls outside fair use or the permission given above, feel free to contact us at *permissions@oreilly.com*.

O'Reilly Online Learning

O'REILLY® For more than 40 years, *O'Reilly Media* has provided technology and business training, knowledge, and insight to help companies succeed.

Our unique network of experts and innovators share their knowledge and expertise through books, articles, and our online learning platform. O'Reilly's online learning platform gives you on-demand access to live training courses, in-depth learning paths, interactive coding environments, and a vast collection of text and video from O'Reilly and 200+ other publishers. For more information, visit *https://oreilly.com*.

How to Contact Us

Please address comments and questions concerning this book to the publisher:

O'Reilly Media, Inc.
1005 Gravenstein Highway North
Sebastopol, CA 95472
800-889-8969 (in the United States or Canada)
707-827-7019 (international or local)
707-829-0104 (fax)
support@oreilly.com
https://www.oreilly.com/about/contact.html

We have a web page for this book, where we list errata, examples, and any additional information. You can access this page at *https://oreil.ly/web-api-cookbook*.

For news and information about our books and courses, visit *https://oreilly.com*.

Find us on LinkedIn: *https://linkedin.com/company/oreilly-media*

Watch us on YouTube: *https://youtube.com/oreillymedia*

Acknowledgments

First of all, a heartfelt thanks to my family and friends for supporting me, especially to my wife, Liz, and son, Benjamin, for putting up with listening to my incessant typing. When I am in the zone, I tend to type very quickly and loudly.

Thank you to Amanda Quinn, Senior Content Acquisitions Editor, for bringing me on as an O'Reilly author. I've read countless O'Reilly books over the years and never thought I'd be writing one of my own one day. Thanks also to Louise Corrigan for making the introduction to Amanda and getting the process started (and who worked with me some years back publishing my very first book!).

Special thanks to Virginia Wilson, Senior Development Editor, for guiding me throughout the process of writing the book and meeting regularly to keep things on track.

I'd also like to thank the fantastic technical reviewers on this book: Martine Dowden, Schalk Neethling, Sarah Shook, and Adam Scott. The book turned out far better with their helpful feedback.

Lastly, I'd like to give a shout out to the teams designing and developing these modern web APIs. Without them, this book would not exist!

CHAPTER 1

Asynchronous APIs

1.0 Introduction

A lot of the APIs covered in this book are *asynchronous*. When you call one of these functions or methods, you might not get the result back right away. Different APIs have different mechanisms to get the result back to you when it's ready.

Callback Functions

The most basic asynchronous pattern is a *callback function*. This is a function that you pass to an asynchronous API. When the work is complete, it calls your callback with the result. Callbacks can be used on their own or as part of other asynchronous patterns.

Events

Many browser APIs are *event* based. An event is something that happens asynchronously. Some examples of events are:

- A button was clicked.
- The mouse was moved.
- A network request was completed.
- An error occurred.

An event has a name, such as `click` or `mouseover`, and an object with data about the event that occurred. This might include information such as what element was clicked or an HTTP status code. When you listen for an event, you provide a callback function that receives the event object as an argument.

Objects that emit events implement the `EventTarget` interface, which provides the `addEventListener` and `removeEventListener` methods. To listen for an event on an element or other object, you can call `addEventListener` on it, passing the name of the event and a handler function. The callback is called every time the event is triggered until it is removed. A listener can be removed manually by calling `removeEventListener`, or in many cases listeners are automatically removed by the browser when objects are destroyed or removed from the DOM.

Promises

Many newer APIs use `Promises`. A `Promise` is an object, returned from a function, that is a placeholder for the eventual result of the asynchronous action. Instead of listening for an event, you call `then` on a `Promise` object. You pass a callback function to `then` that is eventually called with the result as its argument. To handle errors, you pass another callback function to the `Promise`'s `catch` method.

A `Promise` is *fulfilled* when the operation completes successfully, and it is *rejected* when there's an error. The fulfilled value is passed as an argument to the `then` callback, or the rejected value is passed as an argument to the `catch` callback.

There are a few key differences between events and `Promises`:

- Event handlers are fired multiple times, whereas a `then` callback is executed only once. You can think of a `Promise` as a one-time operation.
- If you call `then` on a `Promise`, you'll always get the result (if there is one). This is different from events where, if an event occurs before you add a listener, the event is lost.
- `Promises` have a built-in error-handling mechanism. With events, you typically need to listen for an error event to handle error conditions.

1.1 Working with Promises

Problem

You want to call an API that uses `Promises` and retrieve the result.

Solution

Call `then` on the `Promise` object to handle the result in a callback function. To handle potential errors, add a call to `catch`.

Imagine you have a function `getUsers` that makes a network request to load a list of users. This function returns a `Promise` that eventually resolves to the user list (see Example 1-1).

Example 1-1. Using a Promise-based API

```
getUsers()
  .then(
    // This function is called when the user list has been loaded.
    userList => {
      console.log('User List:');
      userList.forEach(user => {
        console.log(user.name);
      });
    }
  ).catch(error => {
    console.error('Failed to load the user list:', error);
  });
```

Discussion

The `Promise` returned from `getUsers` is an object with a `then` method. When the user list is loaded, the callback passed to `then` is executed with the user list as its argument.

This `Promise` also has a `catch` method for handling errors. If an error occurs while loading the user list, the callback passed to `catch` is called with the error object. Only one of these callbacks is called, depending on the outcome.

Always Handle Errors

It's important to always handle the error case of a `Promise`. If you don't, and a `Promise` is rejected, the browser throws an exception for the unhandled rejection and could crash your app.

To prevent an unhandled rejection from taking down your app, add a listener to the `window` object for the `unhandledrejection` event. If any `Promise` is rejected and you don't handle it with a `catch`, this event fires. Here you can take action such as logging the error.

1.2 Loading an Image with a Fallback

Problem

You want to load an image to display on the page. If there's an error loading the image, you want to use a known good image URL as a fallback.

Solution

Create an `Image` element programmatically, and listen for its `load` and `error` events. If the `error` event triggers, replace it with the fallback image. Once either the requested image or the placeholder image loads, add it to the DOM when desired.

For a cleaner API, you can wrap this in a `Promise`. The `Promise` either resolves with an `Image` to be added or rejects with an error if neither the image nor the fallback can be loaded (see Example 1-2).

Example 1-2. Loading an image with a fallback

```
/**
 * Loads an image. If there's an error loading the image, uses a fallback
 * image URL instead.
 *
 * @param url The image URL to load
 * @param fallbackUrl The fallback image to load if there's an error
 * @returns a Promise that resolves to an Image element to insert into the DOM
 */
function loadImage(url, fallbackUrl) {
  return new Promise((resolve, reject) => {
    const image = new Image();

    // Attempt to load the image from the given URL
    image.src = url;

    // The image triggers the 'load' event when it is successfully loaded.
    image.addEventListener('load', () => {
      // The now-loaded image is used to resolve the Promise
      resolve(image);
    });

    // If an image failed to load, it triggers the 'error' event.
    image.addEventListener('error', error => {
      // Reject the Promise in one of two scenarios:
      // (1) There is no fallback URL.
      // (2) The fallback URL is the one that failed.
      if (!fallbackUrl || image.src === fallbackUrl) {
        reject(error);
      } else {
        // If this is executed, it means the original image failed to load.
```

```
        // Try to load the fallback.
        image.src = fallbackUrl;
      }
    });
  });
}
```

Discussion

The loadImage function takes a URL and a fallback URL and returns a Promise. Then it creates a new Image and sets its src attribute to the given URL. The browser attempts to load the image.

There are three possible outcomes:

Success case
> If the image loads successfully, the load event is triggered. The event handler resolves the Promise with the Image, which can then be inserted into the DOM.

Fallback case
> If the image fails to load, the error event is triggered. The error handler sets the src attribute to the fallback URL, and the browser attempts to load the fallback image. If *that* is successful, the load event fires and resolves the Promise with the fallback Image.

Failure case
> If neither the image nor the fallback image could be loaded, the error handler rejects the Promise with the error event.

The error event is triggered every time there's a load error. The handler first checks if it's the fallback URL that failed. If so, this means that the original URL and fallback URL both failed to load. This is the failure case, so the Promise is rejected.

If it's not the fallback URL, this means the requested URL failed to load. Now it sets the fallback URL and tries to load that.

The order of checks here is important. Without that first check, if the fallback fails to load, the error handler would trigger an infinite loop of setting the (invalid) fallback URL, requesting it, and firing the error event again.

Example 1-3 shows how to use this loadImage function.

Example 1-3. Using the loadImage function

```
loadImage('https://example.com/profile.jpg', 'https://example.com/fallback.jpg')
  .then(image => {
    // container is an element in the DOM where the image will go
    container.appendChild(image);
```

```
}).catch(error => {
  console.error('Image load failed');
});
```

1.3 Chaining Promises

Problem

You want to call several `Promise`-based APIs in sequence. Each operation depends on the result of the previous one.

Solution

Use a chain of `Promise`s to run the asynchronous tasks in sequence. Imagine a blog application with two APIs, both of which return `Promise`s:

`getUser(id)`
> Loads a user with the given user ID

`getPosts(user)`
> Loads all the blog posts for a given user

If you want to load the posts for a user, you first need to load the `user` object—you can't call `getPosts` until the user details are loaded. You can do this by chaining the two `Promise`s together, as shown in Example 1-4.

Example 1-4. Using a `Promise` chain

```
/**
 * Loads the post titles for a given user ID.
 * @param userId is the ID of the user whose posts you want to load
 * @returns a Promise that resolves to an array of post titles
 */
function getPostTitles(userId) {
  return getUser(userId)
    // Callback is called with the loaded user object
    .then(user => {
      console.log(`Getting posts for ${user.name}`);
      // This Promise is also returned from .then
      return getPosts(user);
    })
    // Calling then on the getPosts' Promise
    .then(posts => {
      // Returns another Promise that will resolve to an array of post titles
      return posts.map(post => post.title);
    })
    // Called if either getUser or getPosts are rejected
    .catch(error => {
```

```
      console.error('Error loading data:', error);
    });
}
```

Discussion

The value returned from a Promise's then handler is wrapped in a new Promise. This
Promise is returned from the then method itself. This means the return value of then
is also a Promise, so you can chain another then onto it. This is how you create a
chain of Promises.

getUser returns a Promise that resolves to the user object. The then handler calls
getPosts and returns the resulting Promise, which is returned again from then, so
you can call then once more to get the final result, the array of posts.

At the end of the chain is a call to catch to handle any errors. This works like a try/
catch block. If an error occurs at any point within the chain, the catch handler is
called with that error and the rest of the chain does not get executed.

1.4 Using the async and await Keywords

Problem

You are working with an API that returns a Promise, but you want the code to read in
a more linear, or synchronous, fashion.

Solution

Use the await keyword with the Promise instead of calling then on it (see
Example 1-5). Consider again the getUsers function from Recipe 1.1. This function
returns a Promise that resolves to a list of users.

Example 1-5. Using the await keyword

```
// A function must be declared with the async keyword
// in order to use await in its body.
async function listUsers() {
  try {
    // Equivalent to getUsers().then(...)
    const userList = await getUsers();
    console.log('User List:');
    userList.forEach(user => {
      console.log(user.name);
    });
  } catch (error) { // Equivalent to .catch(...)
    console.error('Failed to load the user list:', error);
```

```
  }
}
```

Discussion

await is an alternative syntax for working with Promises. Instead of calling then with a callback that takes the result as its argument, the expression effectively "pauses" execution of the rest of the function and returns the result when the Promise is fulfilled.

If the Promise is rejected, the await expression throws the rejected value. This is handled with a standard try/catch block.

1.5 Using Promises in Parallel

Problem

You want to execute a series of asynchronous tasks in parallel using Promises.

Solution

Collect all the Promises, and pass them to Promise.all. This function takes an array of Promises and waits for them all to complete. It returns a new Promise that is fulfilled once all the given Promises are fulfilled, or rejects if any of the given Promises are rejected (see Example 1-6).

Example 1-6. Loading multiple users with Promise.all

```
// Loading three users at once
Promise.all([
  getUser(1),
  getUser(2),
  getUser(3)
]).then(users => {
  // users is an array of user objects—the values returned from
  // the parallel getUser calls
}).catch(error => {
  // If any of the above Promises are rejected
  console.error('One of the users failed to load:', error);
});
```

Discussion

If you have multiple tasks that don't depend on one another, Promise.all is a good choice. Example 1-6 calls getUser three times, passing a different user ID each time. It collects these Promises into an array that is passed to Promise.all. All three requests run in parallel.

`Promise.all` returns another `Promise`. Once all three users have loaded successfully, this new `Promise` becomes fulfilled with an array containing the loaded users. The index of each result corresponds to the index of the `Promise` in the input array. In this case, it returns an array with users 1, 2, and 3, in that order.

What if one or more of these users failed to load? Maybe one of the user IDs doesn't exist or there was a temporary network error. If *any* of the `Promises` passed to `Promise.all` are rejected, the new `Promise` immediately rejects as well. The rejection value is the same as that of the rejected `Promise`.

If one of the users fails to load, the `Promise` returned by `Promise.all` is rejected with the error that occurred. The results of the other `Promises` are lost.

If you still want to get the results of any resolved `Promises` (or errors from other rejected ones), you can instead use `Promise.allSettled`. With `Promise.allSettled`, a new `Promise` is returned just like with `Promise.all`. However, this `Promise` is always fulfilled, once all of the `Promises` are settled (either fulfilled *or* rejected).

As shown in Example 1-7, the resolved value is an array whose elements each have a `status` property. This is either `fulfilled` or `rejected`, depending on the result of that `Promise`. If the status is `fulfilled`, the object also has a `value` property that is the resolved value. On the other hand, if the status is `rejected`, it instead has a `reason` property, which is the rejected value.

Example 1-7. Using `Promise.allSettled`

```
Promise.allSettled([
  getUser(1),
  getUser(2),
  getUser(3)
]).then(results => {
  results.forEach(result => {
    if (result.status === 'fulfilled') {
      console.log('- User:', result.value.name);
    } else {
      console.log('- Error:', result.reason);
    }
  });
});
// No catch necessary here because allSettled is always fulfilled.
```

1.6 Animating an Element with requestAnimationFrame

Problem

You want to animate an element in a performant way using JavaScript.

Solution

Use the requestAnimationFrame function to schedule your animation updates to run at regular intervals.

Imagine you have a div element that you want to hide with a fade animation. This is done by adjusting the opacity at regular intervals, using a callback passed to request AnimationFrame (see Example 1-8). The duration of each interval depends on the desired frames per second (FPS) of the animation.

Example 1-8. Fade-out animation using requestAnimationFrame

```
const animationSeconds = 2; // Animate over 2 seconds
const fps = 60; // A nice, smooth animation

// The time interval between each frame
const frameInterval = 1000 / fps;

// The total number of frames for the animation
const frameCount = animationSeconds * fps;

// The amount to adjust the opacity by in each frame
const opacityIncrement = 1 / frameCount;

// The timestamp of the last frame
let lastTimestamp;

// The starting opacity value
let opacity = 1;

function fade(timestamp) {
  // Set the last timestamp to now if there isn't an existing one.
  if (!lastTimestamp) {
    lastTimestamp = timestamp;
  }

  // Calculate how much time has elapsed since the last frame.
  // If not enough time has passed yet, schedule another call of this
  // function and return.
  const elapsed = timestamp - lastTimestamp;
  if (elapsed < frameInterval) {
    requestAnimationFrame(animate);
    return;
  }

  // Time for a new animation frame. Remember this timestamp.
  lastTimestamp = timestamp;

  // Adjust the opacity value and make sure it doesn't go below 0.
  opacity = Math.max(0, opacity - opacityIncrement)
```

```
  box.style.opacity = opacity;

  // If the opacity hasn't reached the target value of 0, schedule another
  // call to this function.
  if (opacity > 0) {
    requestAnimationFrame(animate);
  }
}

// Schedule the first call to the animation function.
requestAnimationFrame(fade);
```

Discussion

This is a good, performant way to animate elements using JavaScript that has good browser support. Because it's done asynchronously, this animation won't block the browser's main thread. If the user switches to another tab, the animation is paused and requestAnimationFrame isn't called unnecessarily.

When you schedule a function to run with requestAnimationFrame, the function is called before the next repaint operation. How often this happens depends on the browser and screen refresh rate.

Before animating, Example 1-8 does some calculations based on a given animation duration (2 seconds) and frame rate (60 frames per second). It calculates the total number of frames, and uses the duration to calculate how long each frame runs. If you want a different frame rate that doesn't match the system refresh rate, this keeps track of when the last animation update was performed to maintain your target frame rate.

Then, based on the number of frames, it calculates the opacity adjustment made in each frame.

The fade function is scheduled by passing it to a requestAnimationFrame call. Each time the browser calls this function, it passes a timestamp. The fade function calculates how much time has elapsed since the last frame. If not enough time has passed yet, it doesn't do anything and asks the browser to call again next time around.

Once enough time has passed, it performs an animation step. It takes the calculated opacity adjustment and applies it to the element's style. Depending on the exact timing, this could result in an opacity less than 0, which is invalid. This is fixed by using Math.max to set a minimum value of 0.

If the opacity hasn't reached 0 yet, more animation frames need to be performed. It calls requestAnimationFrame again to schedule the next execution.

As an alternative to this method, newer browsers support the Web Animations API, which you'll learn about in Chapter 8. This API lets you specify keyframes with CSS properties, and the browser handles updating the intermediate values for you.

1.7 Wrapping an Event API in a Promise

Problem

You want to wrap an event-based API to return a `Promise`.

Solution

Create a new `Promise` object and register event listeners within its constructor. When you receive the event you're waiting for, resolve the `Promise` with the value. Similarly, reject the `Promise` if an error event occurs.

Sometimes this is called "promisifying" a function. Example 1-9 demonstrates promisifying the `XMLHttpRequest` API.

Example 1-9. Promisifying the XMLHttpRequest API

```
/**
 * Sends a GET request to the specified URL. Returns a Promise that will resolve to
 * the JSON body parsed as an object, or will reject if there is an error or the
 * response is not valid JSON.
 *
 * @param url The URL to request
 * @returns a Promise that resolves to the response body
 */
function loadJSON(url) {
  // Create a new Promise object, performing the async work inside the
  // constructor function.
  return new Promise((resolve, reject) => {
    const request = new XMLHttpRequest();

    // If the request is successful, parse the JSON response and
    // resolve the Promise with the resulting object.
    request.addEventListener('load', event => {
      // Wrap the JSON.parse call in a try/catch block just in case
      // the response body is not valid JSON.
      try {
        resolve(JSON.parse(event.target.responseText));
      } catch (error) {
        // There was an error parsing the response body.
        // Reject the Promise with this error.
        reject(error);
      }
    });
```

```
    // If the request fails, reject the Promise with the
    // error that was emitted.
    request.addEventListener('error', error => {
      reject(error);
    });

    // Set the target URL and send the request.
    request.open('GET', url);
    request.send();
  });
}
```

Example 1-10 shows how to use the promisified loadJSON function.

Example 1-10. Using the loadJSON helper

```
// Using .then
loadJSON('/api/users/1').then(user => {
  console.log('Got user:', user);
})

// Using await
const user = await loadJSON('/api/users/1');
console.log('Got user:', user);
```

Discussion

You create a Promise by calling the Promise *constructor function* with the new operator. This function receives two arguments, a resolve and reject function.

The resolve and reject functions are supplied by the JavaScript engine. Within the
Promise constructor, you do your asynchronous work and listen for events. When
the resolve function is called, the Promise immediately resolves to that value. Calling reject works the same way—it rejects the Promise with the error.

Creating your own Promise can help these types of situations, but in general you usually don't need to create them manually like this. If an API already returns a Promise,
you don't need to wrap that in your own Promise—just use it directly.

CHAPTER 2

Simple Persistence with the Web Storage API

2.0 Introduction

The Web Storage API persists simple data locally, in the user's browser. You can retrieve this data later, even after closing and reopening the browser.

This API has a `Storage` interface that provides data access and persistence. You don't create instances of `Storage` directly; there are two global instances: `window.local Storage` and `window.sessionStorage`. The only difference between these is how long they retain the data.

`sessionStorage` data is associated with a specific browser session. It retains the data if the page is reloaded, but closing the browser completely loses the data. Different tabs for the same origin do not share the same persisted data.

On the other hand, `localStorage` shares the same storage space across all tabs and sessions for the same origin. The browser retains this data even after you close the browser. In general, session storage is a good choice if you want to store something ephemeral or sensitive that you want to be destroyed once the browser is closed.

In both cases, storage space is specific to a given origin.

What Is an Origin?

A page's origin is a string combining the protocol (`http` or `https`), host, and port of a URL. For example, the URLs *https://example.com/path/to/index.html* and *https://example.com/profile/index.html* both have the same origin: *https://example.com*.

Getting and Setting Items

Web Storage can only store string values. Each value has a key that you can use to look it up. The API is simple:

getItem(key)
: Returns the string bound to a key, or null if the key doesn't exist.

setItem(key, value)
: Stores a string value under the given key. If the key already exists, you'll overwrite it.

clear()
: Deletes all stored data for the current origin.

Disadvantages

Web Storage can be really useful, but it does have a few disadvantages:

Data storage limitations
: Web Storage can only store string data. You can store simple objects, but not directly—you'll need to convert them to a JavaScript Object Notation (JSON) string first.

Size limitations
: Each origin has a limited amount of space available for storage. In most browsers this is 5 megabytes. If an origin's storage becomes full, the browser will throw an exception if you attempt to add more data.

Security concerns
: Even though the browser stores each origin's data separately, it's still vulnerable to cross-site scripting (XSS) attacks. An attacker can inject code via an XSS attack that steals locally persisted data. Be mindful of what sensitive data you store here.

> The recipes in this chapter all use *local* storage, but they all apply to *session* storage as well, since both objects implement the same Storage interface.

2.1 Checking for Web Storage Support

Problem

You want to check if local storage is available before using it to avoid crashing your app. You also want to handle the situation where local storage is available but blocked by user settings.

Solution

Check the global `window` object for the `localStorage` property to verify that the browser supports local storage. If the check passes, local storage is available (see Example 2-1).

Example 2-1. Checking if local storage is available

```
/**
 * Determines if local storage is available.
 * @returns true if the browser can use local storage, false if not
 */
function isLocalStorageAvailable() {
  try {
    // Local storage is available if the property exists.
    return typeof window.localStorage !== 'undefined';
  } catch (error) {
    // If window.localStorage exists but the user is blocking local
    // storage, the attempt to read the property throws an exception.
    // If this happens, consider local storage not available.
    return false;
  }
}
```

Discussion

The function in Example 2-1 handles both cases: if local storage is supported at all, and if it exists and is not blocked by user settings.

It checks to see if the `window.localStorage` property is not `undefined`. If this check passes, this means the browser supports local storage. If the user has *blocked* local storage, just the act of referencing the `window.localStorage` property throws an exception with a message saying access is denied.

By surrounding the property check with a `try/catch` block, you can also handle this case. When catching the exception, it considers local storage not available and returns `false`.

2.2 Persisting String Data

Problem

You want to persist a string value to local storage and read it back later.

Solution

Use `localStorage.getItem` and `localStorage.setItem` to read and write the data. Example 2-2 shows how we can use local storage to remember the value of a color picker.

Example 2-2. Persisting data to local storage

```
// A reference to the color picker input element
const colorPicker = document.querySelector('#colorPicker');

// Load the saved color, if any, and set it on the color picker.
const storedValue = localStorage.getItem('savedColor');
if (storedValue) {
  console.log('Found saved color:', storedValue);
  colorPicker.value = storedValue;
}

// Update the saved color whenever the value changes.
colorPicker.addEventListener('change', event => {
  localStorage.setItem('savedColor', event.target.value);
  console.log('Saving new color:', colorPicker.value);
});
```

Discussion

When the page first loads, local storage is checked for a previously saved color. If you call `getItem` with a key that doesn't exist, it returns `null`. The return value is only set in the color picker if it is not null or empty.

When the color picker's value changes, the event handler saves the new value to local storage. If there's already a saved color, this overwrites it.

2.3 Persisting Simple Objects

Problem

You have a JavaScript object, such as a user profile, that you want to persist to local storage. You can't do this directly because local storage only supports string values.

Solution

Use JSON.stringify to convert the object to a JSON string before saving it. When loading the value later, use JSON.parse to turn it back into an object, as shown in Example 2-3.

Example 2-3. Using JSON.parse and JSON.stringify

```
/**
 * Given a user profile object, serialize it to JSON and store it in local storage.
 * @param userProfile the profile object to save
 */
function saveProfile(userProfile) {
  localStorage.setItem('userProfile', JSON.stringify(userProfile));
}

/**
 * Loads the user profile from local storage and deserializes the JSON back to
 * an object. If there is no stored profile, an empty object is returned.
 * @returns the stored user profile or an empty object.
 */
function loadProfile() {
  // If there is no stored userProfile value, this will return null. In this case,
  // use the default value of an empty object.
  return JSON.parse(localStorage.getItem('userProfile')) || {};
}
```

Discussion

Passing the profile object directly to localStorage.setItem won't have the desired effect, as shown in Example 2-4.

Example 2-4. Attempting to persist an array

```
const userProfile = {
  firstName: 'Ava',
  lastName: 'Johnson'
};

localStorage.setItem('userProfile', userProfile);

// Prints [object Object]
console.log(localStorage.getItem('userProfile'));
```

The saved value is [object Object]. This is the result of calling toString on the profile object.

`JSON.stringify` takes an object and returns a JSON string representing the object. Passing the user profile object to `JSON.stringify` results in this JSON string (whitespace added for readability):

```
{
    "firstName": "Ava",
    "lastName": "Johnson"
}
```

This approach works for objects like the user profile, but the JSON specification (*https://www.json.org*) limits what can be serialized to a string. Generally speaking, these are objects, arrays, strings, numbers, booleans, and `null`. Other values, like class instances or functions, can't be serialized in this way.

2.4 Persisting Complex Objects

Problem

You want to persist an object that can't be directly serialized to a JSON string, to local storage. For example, the user profile object might have a `Date` object in it specifying when it was last updated.

Solution

Use `replacer` and `reviver` functions with `JSON.stringify` and `JSON.parse` to provide custom serialization for the complex data.

Consider the following profile object:

```
const userProfile = {
    firstName: 'Ava',
    lastName: 'Johnson',

    // This date represents June 2, 2025.
    // Months start with zero but days start with 1.
    lastUpdated: new Date(2025, 5, 2);
}
```

If you serialize this object with `JSON.stringify`, the resulting string has the `lastUpda` ted date as an ISO date string (see Example 2-5).

Example 2-5. Attempting to serialize an object with a `Date` object

```
const json = JSON.stringify(userProfile);
```

The resulting JSON string looks like this:

```
{
  "firstName": "Ava",
  "lastName": "Johnson",
  "lastUpdated": '2025-06-02T04:00:00.000Z'
}
```

Now you have a JSON string that you can save to local storage. However, if you call JSON.parse with this JSON string, the resulting object differs slightly from the original. The lastUpdated property is still a string, not a Date, because JSON.parse doesn't know that this should be a Date object.

To handle these situations, JSON.stringify and JSON.parse accept special functions called replacer and reviver, respectively. These functions provide custom logic to convert nonprimitive values to and from JSON.

Serializing with a replacer function

The replacer argument to JSON.stringify can work in several different ways. MDN has some comprehensive documentation on the replacer function (*https://oreil.ly/ H56TM*).

The replacer function takes two arguments: key and value (see Example 2-6). JSON.stringify first calls this function with an empty string as the key, and the object being stringified as the value. You can transform the lastUpdated field here to a serializable representation of the Date object by calling getTime(), which gives the date as the number of milliseconds since the epoch (midnight UTC on January 1, 1970).

Example 2-6. The replacer function

```
function replacer(key, value) {
  if (key === '') {
    // First replacer call, "value" is the object itself.
    // Return all properties of the object, but transform lastUpdated.
    // This uses object spread syntax to make a copy of "value" before
    // adding the lastUpdated property.
    return {
      ...value,
      lastUpdated: value.lastUpdated.getTime()
    };
  }

  // After the initial transformation, the replacer is called once
  // for each key/value pair.
  // No more replacements are necessary, so return these as is.
  return value;
}
```

You can pass this `replacer` function to `JSON.stringify` to serialize the object to JSON, as shown in Example 2-7.

Example 2-7. Stringifying with the `replacer`

```
const json = JSON.stringify(userProfile, replacer);
```

This generates the following JSON string:

```
{
  "firstName": "Ava",
  "lastName": "Johnson",
  "lastUpdated": 1748836800000
}
```

The number in the `lastUpdated` property is the timestamp for June 2, 2025.

Deserializing with the reviver function

Later, when you pass this JSON string to `JSON.parse`, the `lastUpdated` property remains as a number (the timestamp). You can use a `reviver` function to transform this serialized number value back into a `Date` object.

`JSON.parse` calls the `reviver` function for each property in the JSON string. For each key, the value returned from the function is the value that is set in the final object (see Example 2-8).

Example 2-8. The `reviver` function

```
function reviver(key, value) {
  // JSON.parse calls the reviver once for each key/value pair.
  // Watch for the lastUpdated key.
  // Only proceed if there's actually a value for lastUpdated.
  if (key === 'lastUpdated' && value) {
    // Here, the value is the timestamp. You can pass this to the Date constructor
    // to create a Date object referring to the proper time.
    return new Date(value);
  }

  // Restore all other values as is.
  return value;
}
```

To use the `reviver`, pass it as the second argument to `JSON.parse`, as shown in Example 2-9.

Example 2-9. Parsing with the `reviver`

```
const object = JSON.parse(userProfile, reviver);
```

This returns an object that is equal to the user profile object we started with:

```
{
  firstName: 'Ava',
  lastName: 'Johnson',
  lastUpdated: [Date object representing June 2, 2025]
}
```

Discussion

With this reliable method to convert this object to and from JSON, keeping the `Date` property intact, you can persist these values in local storage.

The approach shown here is just one way to work with a `replacer` function. Instead of a `replacer` function, you could also define a `toJSON` function on the object being stringified. Combined with a factory function, no `replacer` function is necessary.

Factory Functions

Example 2-10 uses a *factory function* to create user profile objects. It takes some arguments and returns a new object containing data based on those arguments. A factory function is similar to a class's constructor function. The main difference is that you use a constructor function with the `new` operator, but a factory is called directly like any other function.

Example 2-10. Using a factory that adds a `toJSON` function

```
/**
 * A factory function to create a user profile object,
 * with the lastUpdated property set to today and a toJSON method
 *
 * @param firstName The user's first name
 * @param lastName The user's last name
 */
function createUser(firstName, lastName) {
  return {
    firstName,
    lastName,
    lastUpdated: new Date(),
    toJSON() {
      return {
        firstName: this.firstName,
        lastName: this.lastName,
```

```
        lastUpdated: this.lastUpdated.getTime();
      }
    }
  }
}

const userProfile = createUser('Ava', 'Johnson');
```

Calling JSON.stringify with the object in Example 2-10 returns the same JSON string as before, with lastUpdated properly converted to a timestamp.

 There isn't any mechanism like this for parsing a string back to an object with JSON.parse. If you use the toJSON approach shown here, you'll still need to write a reviver function to properly deserialize a user profile string.

Since functions can't be serialized, the resulting JSON string won't have a toJSON property. Whatever method you choose, the resulting JSON is the same.

2.5 Listening for Storage Changes

Problem

You want to receive a notification when another tab on the same origin makes changes to local storage.

Solution

Listen for the storage event on the window object. This event fires when other tabs or sessions in the same browser, on the same origin, make changes to any data in local storage (see Example 2-11).

Example 2-11. Listening for storage changes from another tab

```
// Listen for the 'storage' event. If another tab changes the
// 'savedColor' item, update this page's color picker with the new value.
window.addEventListener('storage', event => {
  if (event.key === 'savedColor') {
    console.log('New color was chosen in another tab:', event.newValue);
    colorPicker.value = event.newValue;
  }
});
```

Consider the persistent color picker from Recipe 2.2. If the user has multiple tabs open and changes the color in another tab, you can get notified and update the local in-memory copy of the data to keep everything in sync.

 The storage event is *not* triggered on the tab or page that made the storage change. It's meant to listen for changes that *other* pages have made to local storage.

A storage event specifies which key was changed and what the new value is. It also includes the old value, in case you need it for comparison.

Discussion

The main use case for the storage event is to keep multiple sessions in sync with each other in real time.

 The storage event is only triggered for other tabs and sessions in the same browser on the same device.

Even if you don't listen for the storage event, all sessions on the same origin still share the same local storage data. If you call localStorage.getItem at any point, you'll still get the latest value. The storage event just provides a real-time notification when such a change happens so the app can update the local data.

2.6 Finding All Known Keys

Problem

You want to know all the keys that are currently in local storage for the current origin.

Solution

Use the length property with the key function to build a list of all the known keys. Storage objects don't have a function to return the list of keys directly, but you can build such a list by using the following:

- The length property returns the number of keys.
- The key function, given an index, returns the key at that index.

You can combine these with a `for` loop to build an array of all the keys, as shown Example 2-12.

Example 2-12. Building a list of keys

```
/**
 * Generates an array of all keys found in the local storage area
 * @returns an array of keys
 */
function getAllKeys() {
  const keys = [];

  for (let i = 0; i < localStorage.length; i++) {
    keys.push(localStorage.key(i));
  }

  return keys;
}
```

Discussion

You can combine the `length` property and the `key` function to perform other types of queries, too. This could be, for example, a function that takes an array of keys and returns an object containing just those key/value pairs (see Example 2-13).

Example 2-13. Querying for a subset of key/value pairs

```
function getAll(keys) {
  const results = {};

  // Check each key in local storage.
  for (let i = 0; i < localStorage.length; i++) {

    // Get the ith key. If the keys array includes this key, add it and its value
    // to the results object.
    const key = localStorage.key(i);
    if (keys.includes(key)) {
      results[key] = localStorage.getItem(key);
    }
  }

  // results now has all key/value pairs that exist in local storage.
  return results;
}
```

The ordering of the keys, as referenced with the key function, may not be the same across different browsers.

2.7 Removing Data

Problem

You want to remove some, or all, data from local storage.

Solution

Use the removeItem and clear methods as appropriate.

To remove a particular key/value pair from local storage, call localStorage.removeItem with the key (see Example 2-14).

Example 2-14. Removing an item from local storage

```
// This is a safe operation. If the key doesn't exist,
// no exception is thrown.
localStorage.removeItem('my-key');
```

Call localStorage.clear to remove *all* data from local storage for the current origin, as shown in Example 2-15.

Example 2-15. Removing all items from local storage

```
localStorage.clear();
```

Discussion

Browsers limit the amount of data that you can store in Web Storage. Typically, the limit is about 5 MB. To avoid running out of space and throwing an error, you should remove items once they are no longer needed. Depending on what you're using Web Storage for, you can also provide a way for your users to clear stored data. Consider an emoji picker that stores recently selected emojis in local storage. You might add a Clear Recents button that removes these items.

CHAPTER 3

URLs and Routing

3.0 Introduction

Most web pages and applications deal with URLs in some way. This could be an action like crafting a link with certain query parameters, or URL-based routing in a single-page application (SPA).

A URL is just a string that complies with some syntax rules as defined in RFC 3986, "Uniform Resource Identifier (URI): Generic Syntax" (*https://oreil.ly/SUziR*). There are several component parts of a URL that you may need to parse or manipulate. Doing so with techniques like regular expressions or string concatenation isn't always reliable.

Today, browsers support the URL API. This API provides a URL constructor that can create, derive, and manipulate URLs. This API was somewhat limited at first, but later updates added utilities like the URLSearchParams interface that simplified building and reading query strings.

Parts of a URL

When you call the URL constructor with a string representing a valid URL, the resulting object contains properties representing the URL's different component parts. Figure 3-1 shows the most commonly used of these:

protocol *(1)*
> For web URLs, this is typically http: or https: (note that the colon is included, but not the slashes). Other protocols are possible such as file: (for a local file not hosted on a server) or ftp: (a resource on an FTP server).

`hostname` *(2)*

    The domain or host name (`example.com`).

`pathname` *(3)*

    The path of the resource relative to the root, with leading slash (`/admin/login`).

`search` *(4)*

    Any query parameters. The ? character is included (`?username=sysadmin`).

Figure 3-1. An example URL with its component parts highlighted

Some other parts of the URL include:

`hash`

    If the URL contains a hash, returns the hash portion (including the hash symbol, #). This is sometimes used for internal navigation for older SPAs. For the URL *https://example.com/app#profile*, the value of `hash` would be `#profile`.

`host`

    Similar to `hostname`, but also includes the port number (if specified), for example `localhost:8443`.

`origin`

    The origin of the URL. This usually includes the protocol, hostname, and port (if specified).

You can get the entire URL string by calling `toString` on it, or by accessing its `href` property.

If an invalid URL string is passed to the `URL` constructor, it throws an exception.

3.1 Resolving a Relative URL

Problem

You have a partial or relative URL like `/api/users` that you want to resolve to a full, absolute URL like *https://example.com/api/users*.

Solution

Create a `URL` object, passing the relative URL and the desired base URL, as shown in Example 3-1.

Example 3-1. Creating relative URLs

```
/**
 * Given a relative path and a base URL, resolves a full absolute URL.
 * @param relativePath The relative path for the URL
 * @param baseUrl A valid URL to use as the base
 */
function resolveUrl(relativePath, baseUrl) {
  return new URL(relativePath, baseUrl).href;
}


// https://example.com/api/users
console.log(resolveUrl('/api/users', 'https://example.com'));
```

Without the second argument, the URL constructor would throw an error because /api/users is not a valid URL. The second argument is the base for constructing a new URL. It constructs the URL by assuming the given path is relative to the base URL.

Discussion

The second argument must be a valid URL. To construct the final URL, the typical rules for a valid relative URL are applied depending on the first argument.

If the first argument starts with a leading slash, the pathname of the base URL is ignored and the new URL is relative to the root of the base URL:

```
// https://example.com/api/v1/users
console.log(resolveUrl('/api/v1/users', 'https://example.com'));
```

```
// https://example.com/api/v1/users
// Note that /api/v2 is discarded due to the leading slash in /api/v1/users
console.log(resolveUrl('/api/v1/users', 'https://example.com/api/v2'));
```

Otherwise, the URL is calculated relative to the base URL:

```
// https://example.com/api/v1/users
console.log(resolveUrl('../v1/users/', 'https://example.com/api/v2'));
```

```
// https://example.com/api/v1/users
console.log(resolveUrl('users', 'https://example.com/api/v1/groups'));
```

If the first argument is a valid URL on its own, the base URL is ignored.

If the constructor's second argument is not a string, toString is called on it and the resulting string is used. This means you can pass other URL objects, or even other objects that are similar to URL. You can even pass window.location (a Location object, which has similar properties to a URL) to generate a new URL on the current origin (see Example 3-2).

Example 3-2. Creating a relative URL on the same origin

```
const usersApiUrl = new URL('/api/users', window.location);
```

3.2 Removing Query Parameters From a URL

Problem

You want to remove all query parameters from a URL.

Solution

Create a URL object and set its `search` property to an empty string, as shown in Example 3-3.

Example 3-3. Removing a URL's query parameters

```
/**
 * Removes all parameters from an input URL.
 *
 * @param inputUrl a URL string containing query parameters
 * @returns a new URL string with all query parameters removed
 */
function removeAllQueryParameters(inputUrl) {
  const url = new URL(inputUrl);
  url.search = '';
  return url.toString();
}

// Results in 'https://example.com/api/users'
removeAllQueryParams('https://example.com/api/users?user=sysadmin&q=user');
```

Discussion

The query parameters in the URL are represented in two ways: with the `search` property and the `searchParams` property.

The `search` property is a single string containing all of the query parameters along with the leading ? character. If you want to delete the entire query string, you can set this to an empty string.

Note that the `search` property is set to an empty string. If you set it to `null`, you'll get the literal string `null` in the query string (see Example 3-4).

Example 3-4. Incorrectly trying to remove all query parameters

```
const url = new URL('https://example.com/api/users?user=sysadmin&q=user');

url.search = null;
console.log(url.toString()); // https://example.com/api/users?null
```

The `searchParams` property is a `URLSearchParams` object. It has methods to view, add, and remove query parameters. When adding query parameters, it automatically handles encoding characters. If you want to remove just a single query parameter, you can call `delete` on this object, as shown in Example 3-5.

Example 3-5. Removing a single query parameter

```
/**
 * Removes a single parameter from an input URL
 *
 * @param inputUrl a URL string containing query parameters
 * @param paramName the name of the parameter to remove
 * @returns a new URL string with the given query parameter removed
 */
function removeQueryParameter(inputUrl, paramName) {
  const url = new URL(inputUrl);
  url.searchParams.delete(paramName);
  return url.toString();
}

console.log(
  removeQueryParameter(
    'https://example.com/api/users?user=sysadmin&q=user',
    'q'
  )
); // https://example.com/api/users?user=sysadmin
```

3.3 Adding Query Parameters to a URL

Problem

You have an existing URL that may already have some query parameters in it, and you want to add additional query parameters.

Solution

Use the `URLSearchParams` object, accessible via the `searchParams` property, to add the additional parameters (see Example 3-6).

Example 3-6. Adding additional query parameters

```
const url = new URL('https://example.com/api/search?objectType=user');

url.searchParams.append('userRole', 'admin');
url.searchParams.append('userRole', 'user');
url.searchParams.append('name', 'luke');

// Prints
"https://example.com/api/search?objectType=user&userRole=admin&userRole=user
&name=luke"
console.log(url.toString());
```

Discussion

This URL already has a query parameter (`objectType=user`). The code uses the `searchParams` property of the parsed URL to append a few more query parameters. Two `userRole` parameters are added. When you use `append`, it adds new values and keeps existing values. To replace all parameters of that name with the new value, you can use `set` instead.

With the new parameters, the full URL now is:

```
https://example.com/api/search?objectType=user&userRole=admin&userRole=user
&name=luke
```

If you call `append` with a parameter name but no value, you'll get an exception, as shown in Example 3-7.

Example 3-7. Attempting to call append *without a value*

```
const url = new URL('https://example.com/api/search?objectType=user');

// TypeError: Failed to execute 'append' on 'URLSearchParams':
// 2 arguments required, but only 1 present.
url.searchParams.append('name');
```

This method gracefully handles other argument types. If it doesn't receive a string value, it converts the value to a string (see Example 3-8).

Example 3-8. Appending nonstring parameters

```
const url = new URL('https://example.com/api/search?objectType=user');

// The resulting URL has the query string:
// ?objectType=user&name=null&role=undefined
url.searchParams.append('name', null);
url.searchParams.append('role', undefined);
```

Using `URLSearchParams` to add query parameters automatically handles any potential encoding issues. If you're adding a parameter with a reserved character (as defined in RFC 3986) such as & or ?, `URLSearchParams` automatically encodes these to ensure a valid URL. It uses *percent encoding*, which adds a percent sign followed by the hexadecimal digits representing that character. For example, & becomes %26 because 0x26 is the hex code for an ampersand.

You can see this encoding in action by appending a query parameter containing some reserved characters together, as shown in Example 3-9:

Example 3-9. Encoding reserved characters in a query parameter

```
const url = new URL('https://example.com/api/search');

// Contrived example string demonstrating several reserved characters
url.searchParams.append('q', 'admin&user?luke');
```

The resulting URL becomes:

```
https://example.com/api/search?q=admin%26user%3Fluke
```

The URL contains %26 in place of &, and %3F in place of ?. These characters have special meaning in a URL. ? indicates the beginning of the query string, and & is a separator between parameters.

As Example 3-6 shows, calling `append` multiple times with the same key adds a new query parameter with the given key. When you call `.append('userRole', 'user')`, it adds the parameter userRole=user and keeps the previous userRole=admin. `URLSearchParams` also has a `set` method. `set` adds query parameters as well, but with different behavior. `set` replaces any existing parameters under the given key with the new one (see Example 3-10). If you constructed the same URL again using `set`, the result would be different.

Example 3-10. Adding query parameters with `set`

```
const url = new URL('https://example.com/api/search?objectType=user');

url.searchParams.set('userRole', 'admin');
url.searchParams.set('userRole', 'user');
url.searchParams.set('name', 'luke');
```

When you use `set` instead of `append`, the second `userRole` parameter overwrites the first one, and the resulting URL is:

```
https://example.com/api/search?objectType=user&userRole=user&name=luke
```

Note that there is only one `userRole` parameter—the last one that was added.

3.4 Reading Query Parameters

Problem

You want to parse and list the query parameters in a URL.

Solution

Use the forEach method of URLSearchParams to list the keys and values (see Example 3-11).

Example 3-11. Reading query parameters

```
/**
 * Takes a URL and returns an array of its query parameters
 *
 * @param inputUrl A URL string
 * @returns An array of objects with key and value properties
 */
function getQueryParameters(inputUrl) {
  // Can't use an object here because there may be multiple
  // parameters with the same key, and we want to return all parameters.
  const result = [];

  const url = new URL(inputUrl);

  // Add each key/value pair to the result array.
  url.searchParams.forEach((value, key) => {
    result.push({ key, value });
  });

  // Results are ready!
  return result;
}
```

Discussion

When listing the query parameters on a URL, any percent-encoded reserved characters are decoded back to their original values (see Example 3-12).

Example 3-12. Using the getQueryParameters function

```
getQueryParameters('https://example.com/api/search?name=luke%26ben'); ❶
```

❶ The name parameter contains a percent-encoded ampersand character (%26).

This code prints the parameter `name=luke%26ben` with the original unencoded value:

```
name: luke&ben
```

`forEach` iterates over each unique key/value pair combination. Even if the URL has multiple query parameters with the same key, this prints each unique key/value pair separately.

3.5 Creating a Simple Client-Side Router

Problem

You have a single-page application and want to add client-side routing. This lets the user navigate between different URLs without making a new network request and replacing the content on the client side.

Solution

Use `history.pushState` and the `popstate` event to implement a simple router. This simple router renders the contents of a template when the URL matches a known route (see Example 3-13).

Example 3-13. A simple client-side router

```
// Route definitions. Each route has a path and some content to render.
const routes = [
  { path: '/', content: '<h1>Home</h1>' },
  { path: '/about', content: '<h1>About</h1>' }
];

function navigate(path, pushState = true) {
  // Find the matching route and render its content.
  const route = this.routes.find(route => route.path === path);

  // Be careful using innerHTML in a real app, which can be a security risk.
  document.querySelector('#main').innerHTML = route.content;

  if (pushState) {
    // Change the URL to match the new route.
    history.pushState({}, '', path);
  }
}
```

With this router in place, you can add links:

```
<a href="/">Home</a>
<a href="/about">About</a>
```

history.pushState and the popstate Event

The global `history` object's `pushState` method changes the current URL without reloading the page. It adds the new URL to the browser's history.

The method takes three arguments:

- First, an object containing arbitrary data to associate with the new history entry. This state data is available from the `popstate` event as well.

- The second argument is unused, but must be given. You can use an empty string here.

- Finally, the new URL. This can be an absolute URL, or a relative path. If you use an absolute URL, it must be on the same origin as the current page or the browser throws an exception.

Each call to `pushState` creates a history entry. Whenever the current history entry changes (usually by using the browser's back and forward buttons), the window triggers a `popstate` event.

When you click these links, the browser attempts to navigate to a new page, making a request to the server. This likely results in a 404 error, which is not what you want. To use the client-side router, you need to intercept the click events and integrate with the router from Example 3-13, as shown in Example 3-14.

Example 3-14. Adding click handlers to route links

```
document.querySelectorAll('a').forEach(link => {
  link.addEventListener('click', event => {
    // Prevent the browser from trying to load the new URL from the server!
    event.preventDefault();
    navigate(link.getAttribute('href'));
  });
});
```

When you click one of these links, the `preventDefault` call stops the browser's default behavior (performing a full page navigation). Instead, it takes the `href` attribute and passes it to the client-side router. If it finds a matching route, it renders the content for that route.

To make this a full solution, there is one more necessary piece. If you click one of these client-side routes, then click the browser's Back button, nothing happens. This is because the page isn't actually navigating, but just popping the previous state from the router. To handle this scenario, you need to also listen for the browser's `popstate` event and render the correct content, as shown in Example 3-15.

Example 3-15. Listening for the popstate event

```
window.addEventListener('popstate', () => {
  navigate(window.location.pathname, false);
});
```

When the user clicks the Back button, the browser fires the `popstate` event. This changes the page URL back, and you just need to look up the content for the route matching the URL. In this case, you don't want to call `pushState` because that adds a new history state, which probably isn't what you want since you just popped an old history state off of the stack.

Discussion

This client-side router is working, but there's one issue. If you click the About link, then click the Refresh button, the browser makes a new network request, which probably results in a 404 error. To fix this last problem, the server needs to be configured to return the main HTML and JavaScript content regardless of the URL's pathname. This loads the router code, which is called with the value of `window.location.path name`. If everything is configured right, the client-side route handler executes and renders the correct content.

When using client-side routing, navigating between pages can be faster since there is no round trip to the server. It makes navigation smoother and more responsive. There are disadvantages too. To support the quick page transition, you often have to load a lot of extra JavaScript up front, so the initial page load may be slower.

3.6 Matching URLs to Patterns

Problem

You want to define a pattern of valid URLs that you can match URLs against. You may also want to extract part of a URL's path. For example, given the URL *https://example.com/api/users/123/profile*, you want the user ID (123).

Solution

Use the URL Pattern API to define the expected pattern and extract the part you need.

> This API may not be supported by all browsers yet. See CanIUse (*https://oreil.ly/Eb-k2*) for the latest compatibility data.

With this API, you can create a `URLPattern` object that defines a pattern that you can use to match URLs (see Example 3-16). It's created with a string defining the pattern to match. The string can contain named groups that, when matching against a URL string, are extracted. You can access the extracted values by their index. These groups are similar to capturing groups in a regular expression.

Example 3-16. Creating a `URLPattern`

```
const profilePattern = new URLPattern({ pathname: '/api/users/:userId/profile' });
```

Example 3-16 shows a simple URL pattern with a single named group `userId`. The group name is preceded by a colon character. You can use this pattern object to match URLs and, if they match, extract the user ID from them. Example 3-17 explores some different URLs and how to test them against `profilePattern` using the `test` method.

Example 3-17. Testing URLs against a pattern

```
// The pattern won't match a pathname alone; it must be a valid URL.
console.log(profilePattern.test('/api/users/123/profile'));

// This URL matches because the pathname matches the pattern.
console.log(profilePattern.test('https://example.com/api/users/123/profile'));

// It also matches URL objects.
console.log(profilePattern.test(new URL
('https://example.com/api/users/123/profile')));

// The pathname must match exactly, so this won't match.
console.log(profilePattern.test('https://example.com/v1/api/users/123/profile'));
```

The `profilePattern` specifies an exact pathname match, which is why the last example in Example 3-17 did not work. You can define a less strict version that uses a wildcard character (*) so it needn't be exact. With this new pattern, you can match on partial pathnames.

Example 3-18. Using a wildcard in the pattern

```
const wildcardProfilePattern = new URLPattern
({ pathname: '/*/api/users/:userId/profile' });

// This matches now because the /v1 portion of the URL matches the wildcard.
console.log(wildcardProfilePattern.test
('https://example.com/v1/api/users/123/profile'));
```

You can use the pattern's exec method to get more data about the match. If the pattern matches the URL, exec returns an object containing any matches to parts of the

URL. Each nested object has an `input` property indicating which part of the URL matched, and a `groups` property that has any named groups defined in the pattern.

You can use `exec` to extract the user ID from matching URLs in Example 3-19.

Example 3-19. Extracting the user ID

```
const profilePattern = new URLPattern({ pathname: '/api/users/:userId/profile' });

const match = profilePattern.exec('https://example.com/api/users/123/profile');
console.log(match.pathname.input); // '/api/users/123/profile'
console.log(match.pathname.groups.userId); // '123'
```

Discussion

While it doesn't have full browser support yet, this is a very flexible API. You can define patterns for any parts of the URL, matching inputs and extracting groups.

CHAPTER 4

Network Requests

4.0 Introduction

You'd have a tough time finding a web application today that doesn't send any network requests. Since the dawn of Web 2.0 and the novel approach known as Ajax (Asynchronous JavaScript and XML), web apps have been sending asynchronous requests to get new data without reloading the entire page. The XMLHttpRequest API started a new era of interactive JavaScript apps. Despite the name, XMLHttpRequest (or XHR, as it is sometimes known) can also work with JSON and form data payloads.

XMLHttpRequest was a game changer, but the API can be painful to work with. Eventually, third-party libraries such as Axios and jQuery added more streamlined APIs that wrapped the core XHR API.

In 2015, a newer `Promise`-based API called Fetch became a new standard, and browsers gradually started adding support for it. Today, Fetch is the standard way to make asynchronous requests from your web apps.

This chapter explores XHR and Fetch as well as some other APIs for network communication:

Beacons
    A simple one-way POST request ideal for sending analytics data

Server-sent events
    A one-way persistent connection with a server to receive real-time events

WebSockets
    A two-way persistent connection for bidirectional communication

4.1 Sending a Request with XMLHttpRequest

Problem

You want to send a GET request to a public API, and you want to support older browsers that don't implement the Fetch API.

Solution

Use the XMLHttpRequest API. XMLHttpRequest is an asynchronous, event-based API for making network requests. The general usage of XMLHttpRequest is this:

1. Create a new `XMLHttpRequest` object.

2. Add a listener for the `load` event, which receives the response data.

3. Call `open` on the request, passing the HTTP method and URL.

4. Finally, call `send` on the request. This triggers the HTTP request to be sent.

Example 4-1 shows a simple example of how to work with JSON data using an XHR.

Example 4-1. Making a GET request with XMLHttpRequest

```
/**
 * Loads user data from the URL /api/users, then prints them
 * to the console
 */
function getUsers() {
  const request = new XMLHttpRequest();

  request.addEventListener('load', event => {
    // The event target is the XHR itself; it contains a
    // responseText property that we can use to create a JavaScript object from
    // the JSON text.
    const users = JSON.parse(event.target.responseText);
    console.log('Got users:', users);
  });

  // Handle any potential errors with the request.
  // This only handles network errors. If the request
  // returns an error status like 404, the 'load' event still fires
  // where you can inspect the status code.
  request.addEventListener('error', err => {
    console.log('Error!', err);
  });

  request.open('GET', '/api/users');
  request.send();
}
```

Discussion

The XMLHttpRequest API is an event-based API. When the response is received, a load event is triggered. In Example 4-1, the `load` event handler passes the raw response text to `JSON.parse`. It expects the response body to be JSON and uses `JSON.parse` to turn the JSON string into an object.

If an error occurs while loading the data, the `error` event is triggered. This handles connection or network errors, but an HTTP status code that's considered an "error," like 404 or 500, does *not* trigger this event. Instead, it also triggers the `load` event.

To protect against such errors, you need to examine the response's `status` property to determine if such an error situation exists. This can be accessed by referencing `event.target.status`.

Fetch has been supported for a long time now, so unless you have to support really old browsers you most likely won't need to use XMLHttpRequest. Most—if not all—of the time, you'll be using the Fetch API.

4.2 Sending a GET Request with the Fetch API

Problem

You want to send a GET request to a public API using a modern browser.

Solution

Use the Fetch API. Fetch is a newer request API that uses `Promises`. It's very flexible and can send all kinds of data, but Example 4-2 sends a basic GET request to an API.

Example 4-2. Sending a GET request with the Fetch API

```
/**
 * Loads users by calling the /api/users API, and parses the
 * response JSON.
 * @returns a Promise that resolves to an array of users returned by the API
 */
function loadUsers() {
  // Make the request.
  return fetch('/api/users')
    // Parse the response body to an object.
    .then(response => response.json())
    // Handle errors, including network and JSON parsing errors.
    .catch(error => console.error('Unable to fetch:', error.message));
}

loadUsers().then(users => {
```

```
    console.log('Got users:', users);
});
```

Discussion

The Fetch API is more concise. It returns a `Promise` that resolves to an object representing the HTTP response. The `response` object contains data such as the status code, headers, and body.

To get the JSON response body, you need to call the response's `json` method. This method reads the body from the stream and returns a `Promise` that resolves to the JSON body parsed as an object. If the response body is not valid JSON, the `Promise` is rejected.

The response also has methods to read the body in other formats such as `FormData` or a plain text string.

Because Fetch works with `Promises`, you can also use `await`, as shown in Example 4-3.

Example 4-3. Using Fetch with async/await

```
async function loadUsers() {
  try {
    const response = await fetch('/api/users');
    return response.json();
  } catch (error) {
    console.error('Error loading users:', error);
  }
}

async function printUsers() {
  const users = await loadUsers();
  console.log('Got users:', users);
}
```

> Remember that before using `await` in a function, that function must have the `async` keyword.

4.3 Sending a POST Request with the Fetch API

Problem

You want to send a POST request to an API that expects a JSON request body.

Solution

Use the Fetch API, specifying the method (POST), and the JSON body and content type (see Example 4-4).

Example 4-4. Sending JSON payload via POST with the Fetch API

```
/**
 * Creates a new user by sending a POST request to /api/users.
 * @param firstName The user's first name
 * @param lastName The user's last name
 * @param department The user's department
 * @returns a Promise that resolves to the API response body
 */
function createUser(firstName, lastName, department) {
  return fetch('/api/users', {
    method: 'POST',
    body: JSON.stringify({ firstName, lastName, department }),
    headers: {
      'Content-Type': 'application/json'
    }
  })
    .then(response => response.json());
}

createUser('John', 'Doe', 'Engineering')
  .then(() => console.log('Created user!'))
  .catch(error => console.error('Error creating user:', error));
```

Discussion

Example 4-4 sends some JSON data in a POST request. Calling JSON.stringify on the user object turns it into a JSON *string*, which is required to send it as the body with fetch. You also need to set the Content-Type header so the server knows how to interpret the body.

Fetch also allows you to send other content types as the body. Example 4-5 shows how you would send a POST request with some form data.

Example 4-5. Sending form data in a POST request

```
fetch('/login', {
  method: 'POST',
  body: 'username=sysadmin&password=password',
  headers: {
    'Content-Type': 'application/x-www-form-urlencoded;charset=UTF-8'
  }
})
  .then(response => response.json())
```

```
.then(data => console.log('Logged in!', data))
.catch(error => console.error('Request failed:', error));
```

4.4 Uploading a File with the Fetch API

Problem

You want to upload file data with a POST request, using the Fetch API.

Solution

Use an `<input type="file">` element, and send the file content as the request body (see Example 4-6).

Example 4-6. Sending file data with the Fetch API

```
/**
 * Given a form with a 'file' input, sends a POST request containing
 * the file data in its body.
 * @param form the form object (should have a file input with the name 'file')
 * @returns a Promise that resolves when the response JSON is received
 */
function uploadFile(form) {
  const formData = new FormData(form);
  const fileData = formData.get('file');
  return fetch('https://httpbin.org/post', {
    method: 'POST',
    body: fileData
  })
    .then(response => response.json());
}
```

Discussion

There aren't many steps involved to upload a file using modern browser APIs. The `<input type="file">` provides the file data through the FormData API and is included in the body of the POST request. The browser takes care of the rest.

4.5 Sending a Beacon

Problem

You want to send a quick request without waiting for a response, for example, to send analytics data.

Solution

Use the Beacon API to send data in a POST request. A regular POST request with the Fetch API may not complete in time before the page unloads. Using a beacon is more likely to succeed (see Example 4-7). The browser doesn't wait for a response, and the request is more likely to succeed when sent as the user is leaving your site.

Example 4-7. Sending a beacon

```
const currentUser = {
  username: 'sysadmin'
};

// Some analytics data we want to capture
const data = {
  user: currentUser.username,
  lastVisited: new Date()
};

// Send the data before unload.
document.addEventListener('visibilitychange', () => {
  // If the visibility state is 'hidden', that means the page just became hidden.
  if (document.visibilityState === 'hidden') {
    navigator.sendBeacon('/api/analytics', data);
  }
});
```

A Note on Beacon Reliability

In the past, the recommendation was to use the `beforeunload` or `unload` events to send analytics beacons, but this can be unreliable in many cases. Many sites such as MDN (*https://oreil.ly/iBoG-*) now recommend using the `visibilitychange` event instead.

Discussion

With an `XMLHttpRequest` or `fetch` call, the browser waits for the response and returns it (with an event or `Promise`). In general, you don't need to wait for the response for one-way requests, such as sending analytics data.

Instead of a `Promise`, `navigator.sendBeacon` returns a boolean value that indicates if the send operation was scheduled. There are no further events or notifications.

`navigator.sendBeacon` always sends a POST request. If you want to send multiple sets of analytics data, such as a collection of UI interactions, you can collect them in an array as the user interacts with your page, then send the array as the POST body with the beacon.

4.6 Listening for Remote Events with Server-Sent Events

Problem

You want to receive notifications from your backend server without repeated polling.

Solution

Use the EventSource API to receive server-sent events (SSE).

To start listening for SSE, create a new instance of EventSource, passing the URL as the first argument (see Example 4-8).

Example 4-8. Opening an SSE connection

```
const events = new EventSource('https://example.com/events');

// Fired once connected
events.addEventListener('open', () => {
  console.log('Connection is open');
});

// Fired if a connection error occurs
events.addEventListener('error', event => {
  console.log('An error occurred:', event);
});

// Fired when receiving an event with a type of 'heartbeat'
events.addEventListener('heartbeat', event => {
  console.log('got heartbeat:', event.data);
});

// Fired when receiving an event with a type of 'notice'
events.addEventListener('notice', event => {
  console.log('got notice:', event.data);
})

// The EventSource leaves the connection open. If we want to close the connection,
// we need to call close on the EventSource object.
function cleanup() {
  events.close();
}
```

Discussion

An `EventSource` must connect to a special HTTP endpoint that leaves the connection open with a `Content-Type` header of `text/event-stream`. Whenever an event occurs, the server can send a new message across the open connection.

 As pointed out by MDN (*https://oreil.ly/MliFN*), It's highly recommended to use HTTP/2 with SSE. Otherwise, browsers impose a strict limit on the number of `EventSource` connections per domain. In this case, there can only be up to six connections.

This limit is not per tab; it is imposed across all tabs in the browser on a given domain.

When `EventSource` receives an event over a persistent connection, it is plain text. You can access the event text from the received event object's `data` property. Here's an example of an event of type `notice`:

```
event: notice
data: Connection established at 10:51 PM, 2023-04-22
id: 3
```

To listen for this event, call `addEventListener('notice')` on the `EventSource` object. The event object has a `data` property, whose value is whatever string value is prefixed with `data:` in the event.

If an event does not have an event type, you can listen for the generic `message` event to receive it.

4.7 Exchanging Data in Real Time with WebSockets

Problem

You want to send and receive data in real time without having to repeatedly poll the server with Fetch requests.

Solution

Use the WebSocket API to open a persistent connection to your backend server (see Example 4-9).

Example 4-9. Creating a WebSocket connection

```
// Open the WebSocket connection (the URL scheme should be ws: or wss:).
const socket = new WebSocket(url);
```

```
socket.addEventListener('open', onSocketOpened);
socket.addEventListener('message', handleMessage);
socket.addEventListener('error', handleError);
socket.addEventListener('close', onSocketClosed);

function onSocketOpened() {
  console.log('Socket ready for messages');
}

function handleMessage(event) {
  console.log('Received message:', event.data);
}

function handleError(event) {
  console.log('Socket error:', event);
}

function onSocketClosed() {
  console.log('Connection was closed');
}
```

> To use WebSockets, your server must have a WebSocket-enabled
> endpoint you can connect to. MDN has a nice deep dive on creat-
> ing a WebSocket server (*https://oreil.ly/fzX67*).

Once the socket fires the open event, you can begin sending messages, as shown in
Example 4-10.

Example 4-10. Sending WebSocket messages

```
// Messages are simple strings.
socket.send('Hello');

// The socket needs the data as a string, so you can use
// JSON.stringify to serialize objects to be sent.
socket.send(JSON.stringify({
  username: 'sysadmin',
  password: 'password'
}));
```

A WebSocket connection is a bidirectional connection. Received data from the server
fires a message event. You can handle these as needed or even send a response (see
Example 4-11).

Example 4-11. Responding to a WebSocket message

```
socket.addEventListener('message', event => {
  socket.send('ACKNOWLEDGED');
});
```

Finally, to clean up when you're done, you can close the connection by calling `close` on the WebSocket object.

Discussion

WebSockets are well suited for apps requiring real-time capabilities such as a chat system or event monitoring. WebSocket endpoints have a `ws://` or `wss://` scheme. These are analogous to `http://` and `https://`—one is insecure and one uses encryption.

To initiate a WebSocket connection, the browser first sends a `GET` request to the WebSocket endpoint. The request payload for the URL `wss://example.com/websocket` looks like this:

```
GET /websocket HTTP/1.1
Host: example.com
Sec-WebSocket-Key: aSBjYW4gaGFzIHdzIHBsej8/
Sec-WebSocket-Version: 13
Connection: Upgrade
Upgrade: websocket
```

This initiates a WebSocket handshake. If it's successful, the server responds with a status code of 101 (Switching Protocols):

```
HTTP/1.1 101 Switching Protocols
Connection: Upgrade
Upgrade: websocket
Sec-WebSocket-Accept: bm8gcGVla2luZywgcGxlYXNlIQ==
```

The WebSocket protocol specifies an algorithm to generate a `Sec-Websocket-Accept` header based on the request's `Sec-WebSocket-Key`. The client verifies this value, and at that point the two-way WebSocket connection is active and the socket fires the `open` event.

Once the connection is open, you can listen for messages with the `message` event and send messages by calling `send` on the socket object. Later, you can terminate the WebSocket session by calling `close` on the socket object.

CHAPTER 5

IndexedDB

5.0 Introduction

Chapter 2 covered data persistence with local or session storage. This works well for string values and serializable objects, but querying is not ideal and objects require JSON serialization. *IndexedDB* is a newer, more powerful data persistence mechanism present in all modern browsers. An IndexedDB database contains *object stores* (sort of like tables in a relational database). Each object store can have indexes on certain properties for more efficient querying. It also supports more advanced concepts like versioning and transactions.

Object Stores and Indexes

An IndexedDB database has one or more object stores. All operations to add, remove, or query data are done on an object store. An object store is a collection of JavaScript objects that are persisted in the database. You can define *indexes* on an object store. An index stores extra information to the database that lets you query objects by the indexed property. For example, suppose you are creating a database to store product information. Each product has a key, likely a product ID or SKU code. This lets you quickly search the database for a given product.

If you want to also be able to query the data by price, you can create an index on the price property. This lets you look up objects by their price. With an index, you can specify a specific price or a range of prices, and the index can quickly find those records for you.

Keys

Objects in a store have a *key* that uniquely identifies that object within that store. This is similar to a primary key in a relational database table. There are two types of keys in an IndexedDB object store.

In-line keys are defined on the object itself. For example, here's a to-do item with an in-line key:

```
{
  // Here, id is the key.
  id: 100,
  name: 'Take out the trash',
  completed: false
}
```

Here, the key is the id property. When adding to-do items to such an object store, they must have an id property defined. Additionally, when creating the object store, you would specify a *key path* of id. The key path tells IndexedDB the name of the property that contains the key when using in-line keys:

```
const todosStore = db.createObjectStore('todos', { keyPath: 'id' });
```

If you want to use in-line keys and don't want to worry about maintaining unique keys, you can tell IndexedDB to use auto-incrementing keys:

```
const todosStore = db.createObjectStore('todos',
  { keyPath: 'id', autoIncrement: true });
```

Out-of-line keys are not stored within the object. An out-of-line key is specified as a separate argument with add or put when storing an object. Following the previous example, you could also use out-of-line keys for to-do items. This means the key, or the id property, would not be stored as part of the object:

```
const todo = {
  name: 'Take out the trash',
  completed: false
};

// later, when adding the new to-do
todoStore.add(todo, 100);
```

Transactions

IndexedDB operations use *transactions*. A transaction is a logical grouping of database tasks executed together to perform some work. They are meant to protect the integrity of the data in the database. If one of the operations within a transaction fails, the entire transaction fails and any completed work is rolled back to the state that existed before the transaction.

A transaction can be read-only or read-write, depending on the type of operation you want to perform. You can create a transaction by calling the `transaction` method of an IndexedDB database. You pass the names of any object stores that should be involved in this transaction and the transaction type (`readonly` or `readwrite`).

Once you have a transaction, you can get a reference to the object store(s) you need. From there you can start performing your database operation. These operations return an IndexedDB *request*. All read and write operations in an IndexedDB database require a transaction.

Requests

When you perform an operation on an object store, within a transaction, you'll get back a request object that implements the `IDBRequest` interface, and the requested work begins asynchronously.

When the work is done, the request object triggers a `success` event containing the results. For example, a query operation's `success` event includes the objects found by the query.

Figure 5-1 shows the general flow of an IndexedDB operation: creating a transaction, opening the object store, creating a request, and listening for events.

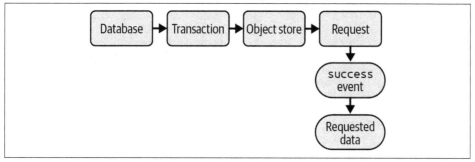

Figure 5-1. The parts of an IndexedDB operation

5.1 Creating, Reading, and Deleting Objects in a Database

Problem

You want to create a basic IndexedDB database where objects can be created, read, and deleted. For example, this could be a contact list database.

Solution

Create a database with a single object store, and define the create/read/delete operations.

To create or open the database, call `indexedDB.open` (see Example 5-1). If the database was not previously created, it triggers an `upgradeneeded` event. In the handler for that event, you can create the object store. When the database is opened and ready for use, it triggers a `success` event.

Example 5-1. Opening the database

```
/**
 * Opens the database, creating the object store if needed.
 * Because this is asynchronous, it takes a callback function, onSuccess. Once the
 * database is ready, onSucces will be called with the database object.
 *
 * @param onSuccess A callback function that is executed when the database is ready
 */
function openDatabase(onSuccess) {
  const request = indexedDB.open('contacts');

  // Create the object store if needed.
  request.addEventListener('upgradeneeded', () => {
    const db = request.result;

    // The contact objects will have an 'id' property that will
    // be used as the key. When you add a new contact object, you don't need to
    // set an 'id' property; the autoIncrement flag means that the database will
    // automatically set an 'id' for you.
    db.createObjectStore('contacts', {
      keyPath: 'id',
      autoIncrement: true
    });
  });

  // When the database is ready for use, it triggers a 'success' event.
  request.addEventListener('success', () => {
    const db = request.result;

    // Call the given callback with the database.
    onSuccess(db);
  });

  // Always handle errors!
  request.addEventListener('error', () => {
    console.error('Error opening database:', request.error);
  });
}
```

Before rendering the contacts, you'll need to load them from the database. For this, use a readonly transaction and call the object store's getAll method, which retrieves all objects in the object store (see Example 5-2).

Example 5-2. Reading the contacts

```
/**
 * Reads the contacts from the database and renders them in the table.
 * @param contactsDb The IndexedDB database
 * @param onSuccess A callback function that is executed when the contacts are loaded
 */
function getContacts(contactsDb, onSuccess) {
  const request = contactsDb
    .transaction(['contacts'], 'readonly')
    .objectStore('contacts')
    .getAll();


  // When the data has been loaded, the database triggers a 'success' event on the
  // request object.
  request.addEventListener('success', () => {
    console.log('Got contacts:', request.result);
    onSuccess(request.result);
  });

  request.addEventListener('error', () => {
    console.error('Error loading contacts:', request.error);
  });
}
```

Adding a contact requires a readwrite transaction. Pass the contact object to the object store's add method (see Example 5-3).

Example 5-3. Adding a contact

```
/**
 * Adds a new contact to the database, then re-renders the table.
 * @param contactsDb The IndexedDB database
 * @param contact The new contact object to add
 * @param onSuccess A callback function that is executed when the contact is added
 */
function addContact(contactsDb, contact, onSuccess) {
  const request = contactsDb
    .transaction(['contacts'], 'readwrite')
    .objectStore('contacts')
    .add(contact);

  request.addEventListener('success', () => {
    console.log('Added new contact:', contact);
    onSuccess();
```

```
  });

  request.addEventListener('error', () => {
    console.error('Error adding contact:', request.error);
  });
}
```

You'll also need a `readwrite` transaction for deleting a contact (see Example 5-4).

Example 5-4. Deleting a contact

```
/**
 * Deletes a contact from the database, then re-renders the table.
 * @param contactsDb The IndexedDB database.
 * @param contact The contact object to delete
 * @param onSuccess A callback function that is executed when the contact is deleted
 */
function deleteContact(contactsDb, contact, onSuccess) {
  const request = contactsDb
    .transaction(['contacts'], 'readwrite')
    .objectStore('contacts')
    .delete(contact.id);

  request.addEventListener('success', () => {
    console.log('Deleted contact:', contact);
    onSuccess();
  });

  request.addEventListener('error', () => {
    console.error('Error deleting contact:', request.error);
  });
}
```

Discussion

When creating the database, you call `indexedDB.open`, which creates a request to open the database. If it triggers an `upgradeneeded` event, you can create the necessary object store.

IndexedDB Versions

IndexedDB has the notion of a *versioned* database. Any time you make changes to your database schema (in the case of IndexedDB, the set of object stores and indexes), you need to consider all the users out there that already have an older version of the database persisted in their browsers.

This is where the `upgradeneeded` event comes in. When you call `indexedDB.open`, you can specify a version number for the database. Each time you modify the schema, you increment this number. If a user with an older version of your database

---

encounters this new version number, IndexedDB triggers the upgradeneeded event. This event tells you the old version and new version of the database. Given these, you can determine what changes you need to make to the database.

This allows your database design to evolve while keeping users' data intact.

Each object in the object store must have a unique key. If you try to add an object with a duplicate key, you'll get an error.

The pattern for the other operations is generally the same:

1. Create a transaction.
2. Access the object store.
3. Call the desired method on the object store.
4. Listen for the success event.

Each of these functions takes an argument called onSuccess. Because IndexedDB is asynchronous, you need to wait until an operation is complete before proceeding. The openDatabase function passes the database to the onSuccess function where you can save it to a variable for later (see Example 5-5).

Example 5-5. Using the openDatabase function

```
let contactsDb;

// Open the database and do the initial contact list render.
// The success handler sets contactsDb to the new database object for later use,
// then loads and renders the contacts.
openDatabase(db => {
  contactsDb = db;
  renderContacts(contactsDb);
});
```

Once you have the contactsDb variable set, you can pass it to the other database operations. When you want to render the contact list, you have to wait until they are loaded first, so you'd pass a success handler that receives the contact objects and renders them (see Example 5-6).

Example 5-6. Loading and rendering contacts

```
getContacts(contactsDb, contacts => {
  // Contacts have been loaded, now render them.
  renderContacts(contacts);
});
```

Similarly, when adding a new contact, you have to wait until the new object is added, then load and render the updated contact list (see Example 5-7).

Example 5-7. Adding and rerendering contacts

```
const newContact = { name: 'Connie Myers', email: 'cmyers@example.com' };
addContact(contactsDb, newContact, () => {
  // Contact has been added, now load the updated list and render it.
  getContacts(contactsDb, contacts => {
    renderContacts(contacts);
  })
});
```

If you don't want to be constantly passing around a database reference, you could encapsulate your database reference and functions inside a new object, as shown in Example 5-8.

Example 5-8. An encapsulated database

```
const contactsDb = {
  open(onSuccess) {
    const request = indexedDB.open('contacts');

    request.addEventListener('upgradeneeded', () => {
      const db = request.result;
      db.createObjectStore('contacts', {
        keyPath: 'id',
        autoIncrement: true
      });
    });

    request.addEventListener('success', () => {
      this.db = request.result;
      onSuccess();
    });
  },

  getContacts(onSuccess) {
    const request = this.db
      .transaction(['contacts'], 'readonly')
      .objectStore('contacts')
      .getAll();

    request.addEventListener('success', () => {
      console.log('Got contacts:', request.result);
      onSuccess(request.result);
    });
  },
```

```
  // Other operations follow similarly.
};
```

With this approach, you still need callbacks to notify you when the operations are done, but the `contactsDb` object keeps track of the database reference for you (and avoids a global variable!).

5.2 Upgrading an Existing Database

Problem

You want to update an existing database to add a new object store.

Solution

Use a new database version. When handling the `upgradeneeded` event, determine if the current user's database needs the new object store to be added based on the version.

Imagine you have a to-do list database with a `todos` object store. Later, in an update to your app, you want to add a new `people` object store so that tasks can be assigned to people.

The `indexedDB.open` call now needs a new version number. You can increment the version number to 2 (see Example 5-9).

Example 5-9. Upgrading a database

```
// todoList database is now at version 2
const request = indexedDB.open('todoList', 2);

// If the user's database is still at version 1, an 'upgradeneeded' event
// is triggered so that the new object store can be added.
request.addEventListener('upgradeneeded', event => {
  const db = request.result;

  // This event is also triggered when no database exists yet, so you still need
  // to handle this case and create the to-dos object store.
  // The oldVersion property specifies the user's current version of the database.
  // If the database is just being created, the oldVersion is 0.
  if (event.oldVersion < 1) {
    db.createObjectStore('todos', {
      keyPath: 'id'
    });
  }

  // If this database has not yet been upgraded to version 2, create the
  // new object store.
```

```
  if (event.oldVersion < 2) {
    db.createObjectStore('people', {
      keyPath: 'id'
    });
  }
});

request.addEventListener('success', () => {
  // Database is ready to go.
});

// Log any error that might have occurred. The error object is
// stored in the request's 'error' property.
request.addEventListener('error', () => {
  console.error('Error opening database:', request.error);
});
```

Discussion

When you call indexedDB.open, you can specify a database version. If you don't specify a version, it defaults to 1.

Whenever the database is opened, the current database version in the browser (if any) is compared with the version number passed to indexedDB.open. If the database doesn't exist yet or the version is not up to date, you'll get an upgradeneeded event.

In the upgradeneeded event handler, you can check the event's oldVersion property to determine the browser's current database version. If the database doesn't exist yet, oldVersion is 0.

Based on the oldVersion, you can determine which object stores and indexes already exist and which need to be added.

If you try to create an object store or index that already exists, the browser throws an exception. Before creating these objects, make sure to check the event's oldVersion property.

5.3 Querying with Indexes

Problem

You want to efficiently query for data based on a property value other than the key (commonly referred to as the "primary key").

Solution

Create an index on that property, then query on that index.

Consider the example of a database of employees. Each employee has a name, department, and a unique ID as its key. You might want to filter the employees by a certain department.

When the `upgradeneeded` event is triggered and you create the object store, you can also define indexes on that object store (see Example 5-10). Example 5-11 shows how to query by the index that is defined.

Example 5-10. Defining an index when the object store is created

```
/**
 * Opens the database, creating the object store and index if needed.
 * Once the database is ready, onSuccess will be called with the database object.
 *
 * @param onSuccess A callback function that is executed when the database is ready
 */
function openDatabase(onSuccess) {
  const request = indexedDB.open('employees');

  request.addEventListener('upgradeneeded', () => {
    const db = request.result;

    // New employee objects will be given an autogenerated
    // 'id' property that serves as its key.
    const employeesStore = db.createObjectStore('employees', {
      keyPath: 'id',
      autoIncrement: true,
    });

    // Create an index on the 'department' property called 'department'.
    employeesStore.createIndex('department', 'department');
  });

  request.addEventListener('success', () => {
    onSuccess(request.result);
  });
}
```

Example 5-11. Querying the employees by the department index

```
/**
 * Gets the employees for a given department, or all employees
 * if no department is given
 *
 * @param department The department to filter by
 * @param onSuccess A callback function that is executed when the employees
```

```
 * are loaded
 */
function getEmployees(department, onSuccess) {
  const request = employeeDb
    .transaction(['employees'], 'readonly')
    .objectStore('employees')
    .index('department')
    .getAll(department);

  request.addEventListener('success', () => {
    console.log('Got employees:', request.result);
    onSuccess(request.result);
  });

  request.addEventListener('error', () => {
    console.log('Error loading employees:', request.error);
  });
}
```

Discussion

An IndexedDB object store can have more than one index, depending on your needs.

This example uses specific values for querying the index, but an index can also be queried for a *range* of keys. These ranges are defined with the IDBKeyRange interface. A range is defined in terms of its *bounds*—it defines a starting and ending point for the range, and all keys within that range are returned.

The IDBKeyRange interface supports four types of bounds:

IDBKeyRange.lowerBound
> Matches keys starting at the given lower bound

IDBKeyRange.upperBound
> Matches keys ending at the given upper bound

IDBKeyRange.bound
> Specifies a lower *and* upper bound

IDBKeyRange.only
> Specifies a single key only

The lowerBound, upperBound, and bound key ranges also accept a second boolean parameter to specify whether the range is open or closed. If true, then it's considered an *open* range and excludes the bounds themselves. IDBKeyRange.upperBound(10) matches all keys less than *or equal to* 10, but IDBKeyRange.upperBound(10, true) matches all keys *less than* 10 because 10 itself is excluded. The bounds for a key range don't have to be numbers. Other object types such as strings and Date objects can be used as keys.

5.4 Searching for String Values with Cursors

Problem

You want to query an IndexedDB object store for objects with a string property matching a pattern.

Solution

Use a cursor, checking each object's property to see if it contains the given string.

Imagine an employee list application. You want to search for all contacts whose name contains the entered text. For this example, assume the database has already been opened and the object store is called `employees`.

A *cursor* iterates through each object in the object store. It stops at each object, where you can access the current item and/or move on to the next item. You can check if the contact name includes the query text and collect the results in an array (see Example 5-12).

Example 5-12. Searching string values with a cursor

```
/**
 * Searches for employees by name
 *
 * @param name A query string to match employee names
 * @param onSuccess Success callback that will receive the matching employees.
 */
function searchEmployees(name, onSuccess) {
  // An array to hold all contacts with a name containing the query text
  const results = [];

  const query = name.toLowerCase();

  const request = employeeDb
    .transaction(['employees'], 'readonly')
    .objectStore('employees')
    .openCursor();


  // The cursor request will emit a 'success' event for each object it finds.
  request.addEventListener('success', () => {
    const cursor = request.result;
    if (cursor) {
      const name = `${cursor.value.firstName} ${cursor.value.lastName}`
        .toLowerCase();
      // Add the contact to the result array if it matches the query.
      if (name.includes(query)) {
        results.push(cursor.value);
```

```
      }

      // Continue to the next record.
      cursor.continue();
    } else {
      onSuccess(results);
    }
  });

  request.addEventListener('error', () => {
    console.error('Error searching employees:', request.error);
  });
}
```

Discussion

When you call `openCursor` on the object store, it returns an `IDBRequest` request object. It fires a `success` event for the first object in the store. For every `success` event, the request has a `result` property that is the cursor object itself. You can access the current value that the cursor is pointing to with its `value` property.

The success handler checks the current object's first and last name fields, converting both to lowercase first so that it's a case-insensitive search. If it matches, it's added to a result array.

When you're done processing the current object, you can call `continue` on the cursor. This advances to the next object and emits another `success` event. If you have reached the end of the object store, and there are no objects left, `request.result` is `null`. When this happens, you know that the search is complete and you have the matching contacts.

At each iteration of the cursor, any objects that match the search query are added to a `results` array. This is passed to the success callback when the cursor is complete.

5.5 Paginating a Large Data Set

Problem

You want to break up a large data set into pages, each with an offset and a length.

Solution

Use a cursor to skip to the first item on the requested page and collect the desired number of items (see Example 5-13).

Example 5-13. Using a cursor to get a page of records

```
/**
 * Uses a cursor to fetch a single "page" of data from an IndexedDB object store
 *
 * @param db The IndexedDB database object
 * @param storeName The name of the object store
 * @param offset The starting offset (0 being the first item)
 * @param length The number of items after the offset to return
 */
function getPaginatedRecords(db, storeName, offset, length) {
  const cursor = db
    .transaction([storeName], 'readonly')
    .objectStore(storeName)
    .openCursor();

  const results = [];

  // This flag indicates whether or not the cursor has skipped ahead to the
  // offset yet.
  let skipped = false;

  request.addEventListener('success', event => {
    const cursor = event.target.result;

    if (!skipped) {
      // Set the flag and skip ahead by the given offset. Next time around,
      // the cursor will be in the starting position and can start collecting
      // records.
      skipped = true;
      cursor.advance(offset);
    } else if (cursor && result.length < length) {
      // Collect the record the cursor is currently pointing to.
      results.push(cursor.value);

      // Continue on to the next record.
      cursor.continue();
    } else {
      // There are either no records left, or the length has been reached.
      console.log('Got records:', request.result);
    }
  });

  request.addEventListener('error', () => {
    console.error('Error getting records:', request.error);
  });
}
```

Discussion

You may not want to start at the first record—that's what the offset argument is for. The first time through, the event handler calls advance with the requested offset. This tells the cursor to jump ahead to the starting item you want. Technically speaking, advance doesn't move to the specified offset but rather advances by the given number *starting at the current index*. For this example, though, it's effectively the same because it always starts at index zero.

You can't start collecting values until the next iteration of the cursor. To handle this, there's a skipped flag that is set to indicate that the cursor has now skipped ahead. The next time through, this flag is seen as true and it won't try to skip again.

Once the cursor has advanced, another success event is fired. Now the cursor is pointing to the first item to be collected (assuming there are items remaining—the cursor object is null if there are no more objects). It adds the current value to the result array. Finally, it calls continue on the cursor to move on to the next value.

This process continues until the result array has reached the requested length, or there are no more objects remaining in the object store. This would happen if offset + length was greater than the number of objects in the object store.

Once there are no more objects to collect, the full page of results is ready.

5.6 Using Promises with the IndexedDB API

Problem

You want a Promise-based API for working with an IndexedDB database.

Solution

Create Promise wrappers around IndexedDB requests. When the request triggers the success event, resolve the Promise. If it triggers the error event, reject it.

Example 5-14 creates a wrapper around the indexedDb.open function. It opens or creates the database and returns a Promise that is resolved when the database is ready.

Example 5-14. Creating a database with a Promise

```
/**
 * Opens the database, creating the object store if needed.
 * @returns a Promise that is resolved with the database, or rejected with an error
 */
function openDatabase() {
  return new Promise((resolve, reject) => {
```

```
    const request = indexedDB.open('contacts-promise');

    // Create the object store if needed.
    request.addEventListener('upgradeneeded', () => {
      const db = request.result;
      db.createObjectStore('contacts', {
        keyPath: 'id',
        autoIncrement: true
      });
    });

    request.addEventListener('success', () => resolve(request.result));
    request.addEventListener('error', () => reject(request.error));
  });
}
```

To load some data from the database, Example 5-15 provides a wrapper around the getAll method. It requests the data, then returns a Promise that is resolved with an array of the objects when they have been loaded.

Example 5-15. Getting objects from a store with a Promise

```
/**
 * Reads the contacts from the database.
 * @returns a Promise that is resolved with the contacts, or rejected with an error
 */
function getContacts() {
  return new Promise((resolve, reject) => {
    const request = contactsDb
      .transaction(['contacts'], 'readonly')
      .objectStore('contacts')
      .getAll();

    request.addEventListener('success', () => {
      console.log('Got contacts:', request.result);
      resolve(request.result);
    });

    request.addEventListener('error', () => {
      console.error('Error loading contacts:', request.error);
      reject(request.error);
    });
  });
}
```

Now that you have an API that returns Promises, you can use then or async/await when working with your database (see Example 5-16).

Example 5-16. Using the promisified database

```
async function loadAndPrintContacts() {
  try {
    const db = await openDatabase();
    const contacts = await getContacts();
    console.log('Got contacts:', contacts);
  } catch (error) {
    console.error('Error:', error);
  }
}
```

Discussion

Using a `Promise` API with `async`/`await` removes the need to pass success handler callbacks around. As Example 5-16 shows, you can also take advantage of `Promise` chaining to avoid nested callbacks and event handlers.

CHAPTER 6

Observing DOM Elements

6.0 Introduction

This chapter looks at three types of *observers* that the browser gives you for watching DOM elements: MutationObserver, IntersectionObserver, and ResizeObserver. These observer objects can watch DOM elements and notify you of certain changes or events.

Observers are created with a callback function. This function is called whenever relevant events occur in the page. It's called with one or more entries that contain information about what occurred. This just creates the observer. To actually start watching an element, you need to call observe on the observer, passing the element you want to observe and an optional set of options.

MutationObserver

MutationObserver watches for changes in the DOM for an element. You can watch for changes to:

- Child elements
- Attributes
- Text content

What the browser observes is defined in an options object passed to the observe function. You can also give an optional subtree option when observing an element. This extends the monitoring of child elements, attributes, and/or text content to all descendant nodes (instead of just the element and its direct children).

When a mutation occurs that you are interested in, your callback gets executed with an array of MutationEntry objects that describe the mutation that just occurred.

ResizeObserver

As its name suggests, ResizeObserver notifies you when an element's size changes. When the size changes, your callback is called with information about what was resized. The entries contain information about the element's new size.

IntersectionObserver

IntersectionObserver watches for changes in an element's position relative to a viewport. The viewport can be a scrollable element or the browser window itself. If any portion of the child element is visible within the scrollable area, it is said to be *intersecting* the ancestor element. Figure 6-1 shows elements on a scrollable page.

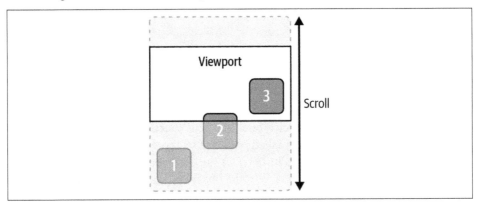

Figure 6-1. Element 1 is not intersecting, element 2 is partially intersecting, and element 3 is fully intersecting

IntersectionObserver uses the concept of an *intersection ratio*—what portion of the element is actually intersecting the root. If the element is fully visible, it has a ratio of 1. If it is completely off-screen, it has a ratio of 0. If it is exactly half visible and half invisible, it has a ratio of 0.5. The entries passed to the callback function have an intersectionRatio property specifying the current intersection ratio.

When you create an IntersectionObserver, you can also specify a *threshold*. This defines when the observer fires. By default, the threshold is 0. This means the observer fires as soon as the element becomes partially visible, even if it's just a single pixel. A threshold of 1 only fires when the element becomes completely visible.

6.1 Lazy Loading an Image When Scrolled into View

Problem

You want to defer loading of an image until its position is scrolled into view. This is sometimes called *lazy loading*.

Solution

Use `IntersectionObserver` on the `<img>` element and wait until it intersects with the viewport. Once it enters the viewport, set the `src` attribute to start loading the image (see Example 6-1).

Example 6-1. Lazily loading an image with `IntersectionObserver`

```
/**
 * Observes an image element for lazy loading
 *
 * @param img A reference to the image DOM node
 * @param url The URL of the image to load
 */
function lazyLoad(img, url) {
  const observer = new IntersectionObserver(entries => {
    // isIntersecting becomes true once the image enters the viewport.
    // At that point, set the src URL and stop listening.
    if (entries[0].isIntersecting) {
      img.src = url;
      observer.disconnect();
    }
  });

  // Start observing the image element.
  observer.observe(img);
}
```

Discussion

When you create an `IntersectionObserver`, you give it a callback function. Every time an element enters or exits, the observer calls this function with information about the element's intersection status.

The observer may be observing multiple elements whose intersection could change at the same time, so the callback is passed an array of elements. In Example 6-1, the observer is only observing a single image element, so the array only has one element.

If multiple elements enter (or leave) the viewport at the same time, there is one entry for each element.

You want to check the `isIntersecting` property to determine if it's time to load the image. This becomes `true` when the element becomes even partially visible.

Finally, you have to tell the observer what element to watch by calling `observe` on the observer object. This starts watching the element.

Once you scroll down enough so that the element enters the viewport area, the observer calls the callback. The callback sets the URL of the image, then stops listening by calling `disconnect`. The callback stops listening because once the image is loaded, there is no need to continue observing the element.

Before `IntersectionObserver`, there weren't many options to do this. One option would be to listen for the parent's `scroll` event, and then calculate if the element is in the viewport by comparing the parent's and child's bounding rectangles.

This, of course, is not very performant. It's also generally considered bad practice. You'd have to throttle or debounce this check to prevent it from running on every scroll operation.

Lazy Loading in Newer Browsers

`IntersectionObserver` has very good browser support, but if you are targeting only newer browsers, there is a way to lazily load images without JavaScript.

In these newer browsers, the `<img>` element supports a `loading` attribute. If this is set to `lazy`, the image won't be loaded until the element is scrolled into the viewport:

```
<img src="/path/to/image.jpg" loading="lazy">
```

You can find the latest data on browser support for the `loading` attribute on CanIUse (*https://oreil.ly/coP8C*).

6.2 Wrapping IntersectionObserver with a Promise

Problem

You want to create a `Promise` that resolves once an element enters the viewport.

Solution

Wrap an `IntersectionObserver` in a `Promise`. Once the element intersects its parent, resolve the `Promise` (see Example 6-2).

Example 6-2. Wrapping an IntersectionObserver with a Promise

```
/**
 * Returns a Promise that is resolved once the given element enters the viewport
 */
function waitForElement(element) {
  return new Promise(resolve => {
    const observer = new IntersectionObserver(entries => {
      if (entries[0].isIntersecting) {
        observer.disconnect();
        resolve();
      }
    });

    observer.observe(element);
  });
}
```

Discussion

When the observer executes your callback with an entry that indicates the element is intersecting, you can resolve the Promise.

As shown in Example 6-3, you could use this approach to lazily load an image, similar to Recipe 6.1.

Example 6-3. Using the waitForElement helper to lazily load an image

```
function lazyLoad(img, url) {
  waitForElement(img)
    .then(() => img.src = url)
}
```

Once you have resolved the Promise, the calling code can be sure the element is in the viewport. At that point the lazyLoad function sets the src attribute on the image.

6.3 Automatically Pause and Play a Video

Problem

You have a <video> element in a scrollable container. When the video is playing, you want to automatically pause it if it scrolls out of view.

Solution

Use IntersectionObserver to watch the video element. Once it no longer intersects the viewport, pause it. Later, if it reenters the viewport, resume it (see Example 6-4).

Example 6-4. Automatically pausing and resuming a video

```
const observer = new IntersectionObserver(entries => {
  if (!entries[0].isIntersecting) {
    video.pause();
  } else {
    video.play()
      .catch(error => {
        // In case of a permission error autoplaying the video.
        // This avoids an unhandled rejection error that could crash your app.
      });
  }
});

observer.observe(video);
```

Discussion

This observer watches the video element. As soon as it scrolls out of view, it is paused. Later, if you scroll it back into view, it is resumed.

Automatically Playing Videos

Browsers are strict about automatically playing videos. If you try to programmatically play a video, like in Example 6-4, the browser may throw an exception. If you don't mute the video by default (by setting the video element's muted attribute), you can't automatically or programmatically play it until the user has interacted with the page.

The play method of the video element actually returns a Promise. To gracefully handle this situation, you should add a call to catch to the Promise.

You shouldn't automatically start playing a video when a page first loads, though. This is annoying and creates accessibility issues. For example, an automatically playing video could be triggering to someone with a vestibular disorder. The audio could also interfere with a screen reader user being able to hear narration.

In a real-world application, you should use this solution only as a convenience once a user has clicked the play button.

6.4 Animating Changes in Height

Problem

You have an element whose contents may change. If the content changes, you want a smooth transition in the height.

Solution

Use a `MutationObserver` to watch the element's children. If the element adds, removes, or changes any child elements, use a CSS transition to smoothly animate the height change. Because you can't animate an element with an `auto` height, this requires some extra work to calculate explicit heights between which to animate (see Example 6-5).

Example 6-5. Animating an element's height due to child element changes

```
/**
 * Watches an element for changes to its children. When the height changes
 * due to child changes, animate the change.
 * @param element The element to watch for changes
 */
function animateHeightChanges(element) {
  // You can't animate an element with 'height: auto', so an explicit
  // height is needed here.
  element.style.height = `${details.offsetHeight}px`;

  // Set a few CSS properties needed for the animated transition.
  element.style.transition = 'height 200ms';
  element.style.overflow = 'hidden';

  /**
   * This observer will fire when the element's child elements
   * change. It measures the new height, then uses requestAnimationFrame
   * to update the height. The height change will be animated.
   */
  const observer = new MutationObserver(entries => {
    // entries is always an array. There may be times where this array has multiple
    // elements, but in this case, the first and only element is what you need.
    const element = entries[0].target;

    // The content has changed, and so has the height.
    // There are a few steps to measure the new explicit height.

    // (1) Remember the current height to use for the animation's starting point.
    const currentHeightValue = element.style.height;

    // (2) Set the height to 'auto' and read the offsetHeight property.
    // This is the new height to set.
    element.style.height = 'auto';
    const newHeight = element.offsetHeight;

    // (3) Set the current height back before animating.
    element.style.height = currentHeightValue;

    // On the next animation frame, change the height. This will
    // trigger the animated transition.
```

```
      requestAnimationFrame(() => {
        element.style.height = `${newHeight}px`;
      });
    });

    // Begin watching the element for changes.
    observer.observe(element, { childList: true });
}
```

Discussion

As with other observers, you need to pass a callback function when you create a `MutationObserver`. The observer calls this function whenever an observed element changes (which changes trigger the callback, specifically, depends on the options passed to `observer.observe`). When your app causes any changes to the element's child list (adding, removing, or modifying elements), the callback recalculates the height to accommodate the new content.

There's a lot going on here, mostly because the browser won't let you animate an element with a `height` of `auto`. To make the animation work, you have to use explicit values for the start and end heights.

When first observing the element, you calculate its height by reading the `offset Height` property. The function then explicitly sets this height on the element. This takes care of the `height: auto` for now.

When the element's children change, the parent won't resize automatically because it now has an explicit height set. The observer callback calculates the new height. With an explicit height set, the `offsetHeight` property has the same value.

To measure the *new* height, you must first set the height *back* to `auto`. Once you do this, `offsetHeight` gives the new height value. However, recall that you can't animate from `height: auto`. Before updating the height, it has to be set from `auto` back to what it was *previously* set to.

At this point you have the new height. The actual height update goes in a call to `requestAnimationFrame`.

This method of calculating the heights adds a lot of extra code. Chapter 8 covers the Web Animations API, which makes these types of animations less painful.

6.5 Change an Element's Content Based on Size

Problem

You want to show different content within an element depending on its size. For example, you may want to handle the case when the element is very wide.

Solution

Use a `ResizeObserver` on the element and update the content if the size goes above or below your defined threshold (see Example 6-6).

Example 6-6. Updating an element's content when it is resized

```
// Look up the element you want to observe.
const container = document.querySelector('#resize-container');

// Create a ResizeObserver that will watch the element for size changes.
const observer = new ResizeObserver(entries => {
  // The observer fires immediately, so you can set the initial text.
  // There's typically only going to be one entry in the array—the first element is
  // the element you're interested in.
  container.textContent = `My width is ${entries[0].contentRect.width}px`;
});

// Start watching the element.
observer.observe(container);
```

Discussion

The `ResizeObserver` calls the callback that you pass every time the element's size changes. The observer also calls it initially when the element is first observed.

The callback is called with an array of `ResizeObserverEntry` objects—here, where you're only observing one element, it's typically going to just be one entry. The `entry` object has a few properties, including `contentRect`, which defines the bounding rectangle of the element. From there you can get the width.

As a result, when the element is resized, the observer callback changes its text to indicate the current width.

 Use care when working with `ResizeObserver` to ensure the code in your callback doesn't trigger the observer again. Such a callback can cause an infinite loop of `ResizeObserver` callbacks. This can happen if you make changes to the element within the callback that cause its size to change again.

6.6 Applying a Transition When an Element Scrolls into View

Problem

You have content that is not initially shown. When the content enters the viewport, you want to show it with an animated transition. For example, when an image scrolls into view, you want to make it fade in by transitioning its opacity.

Solution

Use an `IntersectionObserver` to watch for when the element scrolls into view. When it does, apply the animated transition (see Example 6-7).

Example 6-7. Fading in all images on the page when they scroll into view

```
const observer = new IntersectionObserver(entries => {
  // There are multiple images per row, so there are multiple
  // entries.
  entries.forEach(entry => {
    // Once the element becomes partially visible, apply the animated transition,
    if (entry.isIntersecting) {
      // The image is 25% visible, begin the fade-in transition.
      entry.target.style.opacity = 1;

      // No need to observe this element any further.
      observer.unobserve(entry.target);
    }
  });
}, { threshold: 0.25 }); // Fires when images become 25% visible

// Observe all images on the page. Only images with the 'animate'
// class name will be observed, since you might not want to do this to
// all images on the page.
document.querySelectorAll('img.animate').forEach(image => {
  observer.observe(image);
});
```

Discussion

This recipe uses the `IntersectionObserver`'s `threshold` option. By default, an observer fires as soon as the element becomes visible (a `threshold` of `0`). This isn't ideal here because you want enough of the image to be visible so that the user notices the transition. By setting a `threshold` of `0.25`, the observer won't execute the callback until the image becomes at least 25% visible.

The callback also checks to see if the image is actually intersecting; that is, if it has become visible. This is necessary because when the observer first starts observing an element, it fires immediately. In this case, the images that are offscreen are not yet intersecting, so this check prevents them from becoming visible too early.

If the entry is intersecting, you can set new styles that trigger an animation or transition. In this case, the callback is setting the image's opacity to 1. To make this effect work, you need to have previously set the opacity to 0 and defined a `transition` property of `opacity` (see Example 6-8).

Example 6-8. Styling images to fade in

```
img.animate {
  opacity: 0;
  transition: opacity 500ms;
}
```

With this style, the images are invisible. When the observer callback sets the opacity to 1, the transition takes effect and you'll see the image fade in.

You only want to perform this animation once, so once the image is visible you don't need to observe it anymore. You can clean up by calling `observer.unobserve` and passing the element to stop observing.

6.7 Using Infinite Scrolling

Problem

You want to automatically load more data when the user scrolls to the bottom of a list without the user having to click a Load More button.

Solution

Place an element at the end of the scrollable list and observe it with an `Intersection Observer`. When the element starts intersecting, load more data (see Example 6-9).

Example 6-9. Using `IntersectionObserver` for infinite scrolling

```
/**
 * Observes a placeholder element with an IntersectionObserver.
 * When the placeholder becomes visible, more data is loaded.
 *
 * @param placeholder The Load More placeholder element
 * @param loadMore A function that loads more data
 */
function observeForInfiniteScroll(placeholder, loadMore) {
```

```
  const observer = new IntersectionObserver(entries => {
    // If the placeholder becomes visible, it means the user
    // has scrolled to the bottom of the list. In this case, time to
    // load more data.
    if (entries[0].isIntersecting) {
      loadMore();
    }
  });

  observer.observe(placeholder);
}
```

Discussion

The placeholder element could say Load More, or it can be visually hidden. The IntersectionObserver watches the placeholder element. Once it enters the viewport, the callback starts loading more data. Using this technique, a user can keep scrolling and scrolling until they reach the end of the data.

You could make this placeholder a loading spinner. When the user scrolls to the bottom of the list, triggering a new request, they'll see the spinner while the new data is loading. This is accurate because with the default threshold of 0.0, the observer fires just before the user scrolls far enough to see the spinner. By this time, the data is already loading, so it's not an artificial spinner.

When the observer first starts observing, the callback fires immediately. If the list is empty, the placeholder is visible, which triggers the code to load the first page of data.

CHAPTER 7

Forms

7.0 Introduction

Forms collect user input that is submitted to a remote URL or API endpoint. Modern browsers have many built-in form input types for text, numbers, colors, and more. A form is one of the main ways you get input from your user.

FormData

The FormData API provides a data model for accessing form data. It saves you the trouble of having to look up individual DOM elements and get their values.

Even better, once you have a FormData object, you can pass it directly to the Fetch API to submit the form. Before submission, you can alter or add to the data in the FormData object.

Validation

To prevent users from sending invalid data, you can (and should) add client-side validation for your forms. This could be something as simple as marking a field as required, or more complex validation logic that involves coordinating multiple form values or calling an API.

In the past, a developer would usually need to reach for a JavaScript library to perform form validation. This could cause headaches due to data duplication; it exists in the form data and an in-memory object used by the validation library.

HTML5 added more built-in validation options, such as:

- Marking a field as required
- Specifying the minimum and maximum values in a number field
- Specifying a regular expression to validate the field's input

These options are used as attributes on the `<input>` elements.

The browser shows basic validation error messages (see Figure 7-1), but the style may not look good with your app's design. You can use the Constraint Validation API to inspect the built-in validation results as well as perform custom validation logic and set your own validation messages.

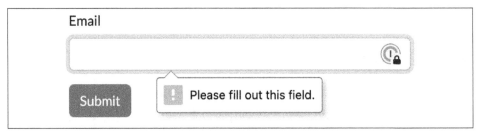

Figure 7-1. A built-in validation message in Chrome

To validate a form, you call its `checkValidity` method. All of the fields within the form are validated. If all fields are valid, `checkValidity` returns `true`. If one or more fields are invalid, `checkValidity` returns `false` and each invalid field triggers an `invalid` event. You can also check a specific element by calling `checkValidity` on the form field itself.

Every form field has a `validity` object that reflects the current validity state. It has a boolean `valid`, which indicates the form's overall validity state. This object also has additional flags that tell you the nature of the validation error.

7.1 Populating a Form Field from Local Storage

Problem

You want to remember a form field's value in local storage. For example, you may want to remember the user name entered in a login form.

Solution

When submitting the form, use a `FormData` object to get the field value and set it in local storage (see Example 7-1). Then, when first loading the page, check for a remembered value. If you find a value, populate the form field.

Example 7-1. Remembering the username field

```
const form = document.querySelector('#login-form');

const username = localStorage.getItem('username');
if (username) {
  form.elements.username.value = username;
}

form.addEventListener('submit', event => {
  const data = new FormData(form);
  localStorage.setItem('username', data.get('username'));
});
```

Discussion

When you pass a form to the `FormData` constructor, it is populated with the form's current values. You can then use the `get` method to retrieve the desired field and set it in local storage.

Populating the form on load is a little different. A `FormData` object is not kept in sync with the current form values; rather, it includes the form values at the time the `FormData` object was created. The opposite is also true—if you set a new value in the `FormData` object, it won't be updated in the form itself. Given this, a `FormData` object won't help when populating the form. Example 7-1 uses the form's `elements` property to look up the `username` field and set its value that way.

Looking Up Form Fields with the elements Property

The `elements` property of a form lets you look up form fields by their names. Every field within this form that has a `name` property has a corresponding property in `form.elements`. For example, you can look up an input with the name `username` by referencing `form.elements.username`. Note that you need to specify the field's `name` attribute, not its `id`.

7.2 Submitting a Form with Fetch and the FormData API

Problem

You want to submit a form using the Fetch API. You might want to do this to add additional information to the form submission that wouldn't be included by the browser, or because the form submission might need an API token that is stored in memory rather than entered in the form.

Another reason you might want to do this is to prevent the browser from redirecting to a new page, or causing a full page refresh.

Solution

Create a `FormData` object containing the data to be submitted. Add the additional required data, then submit the form with the Fetch API (see Example 7-2).

Example 7-2. Adding data with the FormData API

```
// In a real-world application, the API token would be stored somewhere and
// not hardcoded like this.
const apiToken = 'aBcD1234EfGh5678IjKlM';

form.addEventListener('submit', event => {
  // Important: Stop the browser from automatically submitting the form.
  event.preventDefault();

  // Set up a FormData object and add the API token to it.
  const data = new FormData(event.target);
  data.set('apiToken', apiToken);

  // Use the Fetch API to send this FormData object to the endpoint.
  fetch('/api/form', {
    method: 'POST',
    body: data
  });
});
```

Discussion

Normally, when you click the Submit button, the browser gets the form data and submits it for you. Here you don't want that because you need to add the API token.

The first thing the submit handler does is call `preventDefault` on the `submit` event. This stops the browser from performing the default submit behavior so that you can provide your custom logic. The default behavior here is a full page refresh, which is probably not what you want.

You can create a `FormData` object by passing the form object to the `FormData` constructor. The resulting object will have the existing form data in it, at which point you can add additional data like the API token.

Finally, you can pass the `FormData` object as the body of a POST request using the Fetch API. When submitting a form this way, the body is *not* JSON; rather, the browser submits it with a content type of `multipart/form-data`.

Consider an object representing your form data:

```
{
  username: 'john.doe',
  apiToken: 'aBcD1234EfGh5678IjKlM'
}
```

The equivalent request body looks something like this:

```
------WebKitFormBoundaryl6AuUOn9EbuYe9XO
Content-Disposition: form-data; name="username"

john.doe
------WebKitFormBoundaryl6AuUOn9EbuYe9XO
Content-Disposition: form-data; name="apiToken"

aBcD1234EfGh5678IjKlM
------WebKitFormBoundaryl6AuUOn9EbuYe9XO--
```

7.3 Submitting a Form as JSON

Problem

You want to submit a form to an endpoint that expects JSON data.

Solution

Use the FormData API to transform the form data into a JavaScript object, and use the Fetch API to send it as JSON (see Example 7-3).

Example 7-3. Submitting a form as JSON using Fetch

```
form.addEventListener('submit', event => {
  // Important: Stop the browser from automatically submitting the form.
  event.preventDefault();

  // Create a new FormData containing this form's data, then add each
  // key/value pair to the response body.
  const data = new FormData(event.target);
  const body = {};
  for (const [key, value] of data.entries()) {
    body[key] = value;
```

```
  }

  // Send the JSON body to the form endpoint.
  fetch('/api/form', {
    method: 'POST',

    // The object must be converted to a JSON string.
    body: JSON.stringify(body),

    // Tell the server you're sending JSON.
    headers: {
      'content-type': 'application/json'
    }
  })
    .then(response => response.json())
    .then(body => console.log('Got response:', body));
});
```

Discussion

This approach is similar to sending the FormData object directly. The only differences are that you are converting the form data to JSON and sending it with the correct Content-Type header.

You can perform the conversion by creating a new empty object and iterating over the key/value pairs in the FormData. Each pair is copied into the object.

A disadvantage of this approach is that you can't use it with FormData having multiple values bound to the same key. This happens when you have a group of checkboxes with the same name; there are multiple entries with the same key.

You could enhance the conversion to detect this case and set an array of values, as shown in Example 7-4.

Example 7-4. Handling array form values

```
/**
 * Converts a form's data into an object that can be sent as JSON.
 * @param form The form element
 * @returns An object containing all the mapped keys and values
 */
function toObject(form) {
  const data = new FormData(form);
  const body = {};

  for (const key of data.keys()) {
    // Returns an array of all values bound to a given key
    const values = data.getAll(key);

    // If there's only one element in the array, set that element directly.
```

```
    if (values.length === 1) {
      body[key] = values[0];
    } else {
      // Otherwise, set the array
      body[key] = values;
    }
  }

  return body;
}
```

Example 7-4 uses the FormData's getAll function, which returns an array containing all values bound to the given key. This lets you collect all values for a given checkbox group into an array.

getAll always returns an array. If there's only one value, it is an array with one element. toObject checks for this scenario, and if the array only has one element, it uses that element as the single value in the resulting object. Otherwise, it uses the array of values.

7.4 Making a Form Field Required

Problem

You want to require a form field to have a value, causing a validation error if it is left blank.

Solution

Use the required attribute on the <input> element (see Example 7-5).

Example 7-5. A required field

```
<label for="username">Username</label>
<input type="text" name="username" id="username" required> ❶
```

❶ The required attribute does not have a value.

Discussion

When a field is marked as required, it must have a value. If the field is blank, its validity.valid property is false and its validity.valueMissing property is true.

A required field is only considered empty if the value is an empty string. It does not trim whitespace, so a value consisting of a few empty spaces is considered valid.

7.5 Constraining a Number Input

Problem

You want to specify a range of allowed values for a number input (`<input type= "number">`).

Solution

Use the `min` and `max` properties to specify the allowed range (see Example 7-6). These values are inclusive, meaning that the minimum and maximum values themselves are allowed.

Example 7-6. Specifying a range for a number field

```
<label for="quantity">Quantity</label>
<input type="number" name="quantity" id="quantity" min="1" max="10">
```

Discussion

If a number input's value is below the minimum or above the maximum, its `validity.valid` property is `false`. If it's below the minimum, the `rangeUnderflow` validity flag is set. Similarly, if it exceeds the maximum, the `rangeOverflow` flag is set instead.

When you make an `input` of type `number`, the browser adds a spinner control—clickable up and down arrows to increase and decrease the value. This spinner control enforces the minimum and maximum values—it refuses to decrease the value if it's already at the minimum or increase the value if it's already at the maximum. However, a user is still free to type any value in the field. They can enter a number outside of the allowed range, at which point the validity state is set accordingly.

If you want more fine-grained control over allowed values, you can also specify a `step` value. This limits the allowed values so that the increment must be a multiple of the step. Consider an input with a minimum of 0, a maximum of 4, and a step of 2. The only acceptable values for this field would be 0, 2, and 4.

7.6 Specifying a Validation Pattern

Problem

You want to limit a text field's value so that it matches a certain pattern.

Solution

Use the `pattern` attribute of the `input` to specify a regular expression (see Example 7-7). The field is considered invalid unless its value matches the regular expression.

Example 7-7. Limiting a field to alphanumeric characters only

```
<label for="username">Enter a username</label>
<input type="text" pattern="[A-Za-z0-9]+" id="username" name="username">
```

The `username` field is invalid if it contains anything other than alphanumeric characters. When invalid, the validity state's `patternMismatch` flag is set.

Discussion

This is a flexible validation option, second only to using your own custom validation logic (see Recipe 7.8).

Creating a regular expression to validate URLs or email addresses can be tricky. To handle these cases, you can set the input's `type` attribute to `url` or `email`, and the browser will validate that the field is a valid URL or email address for you.

7.7 Validating Forms

Problem

You want to manage the form validation process and show your own error messages in the UI.

Solution

Use the Constraint Validation API and the `invalid` event to detect and mark invalid fields.

There are many ways to handle validation. Some websites are too eager and show an error message before the user gets a chance to enter a value. Consider an input of type `email`, which is considered invalid until a valid email address is entered. If validation occurs immediately, the user sees an error about an invalid email address before they've even finished typing it.

To avoid this, the validation approach shown here only validates a field under two conditions:

- When the form is submitted.
- If the field has been focused and then lost focus. These fields are considered to have been "touched."

First, you'll need to disable the browser's built-in validation UI by adding the `novalidate` attribute to the form, as shown in Example 7-8.

Example 7-8. Disabling the browser validation UI

```
<form id="my-form" novalidate>
  <!-- Form elements go here -->
</form>
```

Each field needs a placeholder element to contain the error message, as shown in Example 7-9.

Example 7-9. Adding error message placeholders

```
<div>
  <label for="email">Email</label>
  <input required type="email" id="email" name="email">
  <div class="error-message" id="email-error"></div>
</div>
```

In this example, an error message is associated with an input field by its ID. The field with the ID `email` has an error message with ID `email-error`, a `name` field has an error message `name-error`, and so on.

With this validation approach, each form element listens for three events:

`invalid`

Triggered when the form is validated and the field is marked invalid. This sets the error message.

`input`

Triggered when the value in the field changes. This performs revalidation if necessary and clears the error message if the field becomes valid.

`blur`

Triggered when the field loses focus. This sets a `data-should-validate` attribute to mark the field as touched, after which it is validated in the `input` event handler.

The validation code is shown in Example 7-10.

Example 7-10. Setting up validation for a form field

```
/**
 * Adds necessary event listeners to an element to participate in form validation.
 * It handles setting and clearing error messages depending on the validation state.
 * @param element The input element to validate
 */
function addValidation(element) {
  const errorElement = document.getElementById(`${element.id}-error`);

  /**
   * Fired when the form is validated and the field is not valid.
   * Sets the error message and style, and also sets the shouldValidate flag.
   */
  element.addEventListener('invalid', () => {
    errorElement.textContent = element.validationMessage;
    element.dataset.shouldValidate = true;
  });

  /**
   * Fired when user input occurs in the field. If the shouldValidate flag is set,
   * it will recheck the field's validity and clear the error message if it
   * becomes valid.
   */
  element.addEventListener('input', () => {
    if (element.dataset.shouldValidate) {
      if (element.checkValidity()) {
        errorElement.textContent = '';
      }
    }
  });

  /**
   * Fired when the field loses focus, applying the shouldValidate flag.
   */
  element.addEventListener('blur', () => {
    // This field has been touched; it will now be validated on subsequent
    // 'input' events.
    // This sets the input's data-should-validate attribute to true in the DOM.
    element.dataset.shouldValidate = true;
  });
}
```

This example listens to the `input` event. If your form contains checkboxes or radio buttons, you may need to listen for the `change` event instead for those elements, depending on the browser. See the article about input events from MDN (*https://oreil.ly/cFIjY*):

> For `<input>` elements with type=checkbox or type= radio, the `input` event should fire whenever a user toggles the control, per the HTML Living Standard specification. However, historically this has not always been the case. Check compatibility, or use the `change` event instead for elements of these types.

To complete the basic validation framework, add the listeners to the form fields, listen for the form's `submit` event, and trigger validation (see Example 7-11).

Example 7-11. Triggering form validation

```
// Assuming the form has two inputs, 'name' and 'email'
addValidation(form.elements.name);
addValidation(form.elements.email);

form.addEventListener('submit', event => {
  event.preventDefault();
  if (form.checkValidity()) {
    // Validation passed, submit the form
  }
});
```

Discussion

This code sets up a good basic validation framework that handles the browser's built-in validation. Before submitting the form, it calls `checkValidity`, which starts checking all of the inputs inside the form. The browser triggers an `invalid` event for any input that fails validation. To handle this, you can listen for the `invalid` event on the input elements themselves. From there, you can render an appropriate error message.

Once the user has validation errors, you want to clear them as soon as the fields become valid. This is why `addValidation` listens for the `input` event—this is triggered as soon as the user types something in the input field. From there, you can immediately recheck the input's validity. If it is now valid (`checkValidity` returns true), you can clear the error message. An input is only revalidated if the `data-should-validate` attribute is set to `true`. This attribute is added when validation fails during form submission, or when an element loses focus. This prevents validation errors from appearing before the user is done typing. Once the field loses focus, it starts revalidating on every change.

7.8 Using Custom Validation Logic

Problem

You want to perform a validation check that is not supported by the Constraint Validation API. For example, you want to validate that a password and password confirmation field have the same value.

Solution

Perform the custom validation logic before calling `checkValidity` on the form. If the custom validation check fails, call the input's `setCustomValidity` method to set an appropriate error message. If the check passes, clear any previously set validation message (see Example 7-12).

Example 7-12. Using custom validation

```
/**
 * Custom validation function that ensures the password and confirmPassword fields
 * have the same value.
 * @param form The form containing the two fields
 */
function validatePasswordsMatch(form) {
  const { password, confirmPassword } = form.elements;

  if (password.value !== confirmPassword.value) {
    confirmPassword.setCustomValidity('Passwords do not match.');
  } else {
    confirmPassword.setCustomValidity('');
  }
}

form.addEventListener('submit', event => {
  event.preventDefault();

  validatePasswordsMatch(form);
  if (form.checkValidity()) {
    // Validation passed, submit the form.
  }
});
```

If you're using the browser's built-in validation UI, you need to call the form field's `reportValidity` method after setting a custom validity message. If you are handling the validation UI yourself, this isn't needed—but make sure to show the error message in the appropriate place.

Discussion

When you call `setCustomValidity` on an element with a non-empty string, the element is now considered invalid.

The `validatePasswordsMatch` function examines the values of the `password` and `confirmPassword` fields. If they don't match, it calls `setCustomValidity` on the `confirmPassword` field to set a validation error message. If they do match, it sets it to an empty string, which marks the field as valid again.

The form's submit handler calls `validatePasswordsMatch` before performing the built-in validation. If the `validatePasswordsMatch` check fails, and a custom validity is set, `form.checkValidity` fails and the `invalid` event fires on the `confirmPassword` field just like any other invalid element.

7.9 Validating a Checkbox Group

Problem

You want to enforce that at least one checkbox in a group of checkboxes must be checked. Setting the `required` attribute on checkboxes won't help here because it applies to that individual input only, not the group. The browser checks if that input is checked and causes a validation error, even if other checkboxes in the group are checked.

Solution

Use a `FormData` object to get an array of all selected checkboxes, and set a custom validation error if the array is empty.

When performing the custom validation, use the `FormData`'s `getAll` method to get an array of the selected checkbox values (see Example 7-13). If the array is empty, no checkboxes are selected, and this is a validation error.

Example 7-13. Validating a checkbox group

```
function validateCheckboxes(form) {
  const data = new FormData(form);

  // To avoid setting the validation error on multiple elements,
  // choose the first checkbox and use that to hold the group's validation
  // message.
  const element = form.elements.option1;

  if (!data.has('options')) {
    element.setCustomValidity('Please select at least one option.');
```

```
  } else {
    element.setCustomValidity('');
  }
}
```

To keep the validation state of the whole group in one place, set the custom validity message on the first checkbox only (assuming a name of option1). This first checkbox serves as a container for the group's validation message, which is necessary because you can only set validity messages on actual <input> elements.

Then, listen for the invalid and change events. On the invalid event, show the error message. On the change event (when a checkbox is toggled), perform the custom validation and clear the error message if validation succeeds (see Example 7-14).

Example 7-14. Setting up checkbox validation

```
/**
 * Adds necessary event listeners to an element to participate in form validation.
 * It handles setting and clearing error messages depending on the validation state.
 * @param element The input element to validate
 * @param errorId The ID of a placeholder element that will show the error message
 */
function addValidation(element, errorId) {
  const errorElement = document.getElementById(errorId);

  /**
   * Fired when the form is validated and the field is not valid.
   * Sets the error message and style.
   */
  element.addEventListener('invalid', () => {
    errorElement.textContent = element.validationMessage;
  });

  /**
   * Fired when user input occurs in the field.
   * It will recheck the field's validity and clear the error message if it
   * becomes valid.
   */
  element.addEventListener('change', () => {
    validateCheckboxes(form);
    if (form.elements.option1.checkValidity()) {
      errorElement.textContent = '';
    }
  });
}
```

Finally, add validation to each checkbox field and call the `validateCheckboxes` function before checking the form's validity. Example 7-15 expects that you have an element with the ID `checkbox-error`. If there is a checkbox validation error, the message will be set on that element.

Example 7-15. Validating the checkbox form

```
addValidation(form.elements.option1, 'checkbox-error');
addValidation(form.elements.option2, 'checkbox-error');
addValidation(form.elements.option3, 'checkbox-error');

form.addEventListener('submit', event => {
  event.preventDefault();
  validateCheckboxes(form);
  console.log(form.checkValidity());
});
```

Discussion

Using the `required` attribute on the checkboxes in the group won't have the desired effect. This is good for a single checkbox, like one requiring that a user accept a license agreement, but when used on a group, it would make each individual checkbox required, and form validation would fail unless *all* of them were checked. Because there is no HTML element for a "checkbox group," you'll need to do a little extra work to get the desired behavior.

This example picks the first checkbox in the group as a "container" for the validation message. When the user toggles any of the checkboxes, the browser calls the change handler and it looks to see if any of the checkboxes are checked. If the selection array is empty, this is an error. The custom validity message is always set on the first checkbox only. This is to ensure the message is always shown and hidden when necessary.

Let's look at what would happen if you instead applied the custom validity to the checkbox being changed.

If no options are checked and the user submits the form, each checkbox has a custom validity error message now. All three options are invalid. If you then go and check one of the checkboxes, the checkbox's `change` event will fire and check the checkbox group. Now there is an option selected, so it clears the custom validity message. However, the other checkboxes are still in an error state. This is essentially now equivalent to having set the `required` attribute on all the checkboxes.

You could get around this by setting the validation message in *all* checkboxes from the `validateCheckboxes` function, but it's less work to just pick one and use that as the target for all custom validation messages. The group as a whole has a single error message element that gets populated with the validation error.

Since this example manages its own validation message, make sure to include the `novalidate` attribute on the containing form to avoid showing the browser's default validation UI along with your custom validation error.

7.10 Validating a Field Asynchronously

Problem

Your custom validation logic requires an asynchronous operation like making a network request. For example, a user signup form has a password field. The signup form must call an API to validate that the entered password meets password strength standards.

Solution

Perform the network request, then set a custom validity message. Do this in a function that returns a `Promise`. In the form's submit handler, await this `Promise` before calling `checkValidity` on the form. If the asynchronous validation code set a custom validity message, the form validation triggered by `checkValidity` handles it.

Example 7-16 has the validation logic itself. It calls a password strength check API and sets the custom validity message accordingly.

Example 7-16. Performing asynchronous password strength validation

```
/**
 * Calls an API to validate that a password meets strength requirements.
 * @param form The form containing the password field
 */
async function validatePasswordStrength(form) {
  const { password } = form.elements;
  const response = await fetch(`/api/password-strength?password=${password.value}`);
  const result = await response.json();

  // As before, remember to call reportValidity on the password field if you're using
  // the built-in browser validation UI.
  if (result.status === 'error') {
    password.setCustomValidity(result.error);
  } else {
    password.setCustomValidity('');
  }
}
```

Make sure you only send passwords over a secure connection (HTTPS). Otherwise, you're sending the user's password out in plain text, and this is a dangerous practice.

Because the function is marked as `async`, it returns a `Promise`. You just need to `await` this `Promise` in the form's submit handler, as shown in Example 7-17.

Example 7-17. The async form submit handler

```
form.addEventListener('submit', async event => {
  event.preventDefault();
  await validatePasswordStrength(form);
  console.log(form.checkValidity());
});
```

This marks the field as invalid on submission if the password doesn't meet the requirements. You can rerun the validation logic when the field changes, only this time you'll do it on the `blur` event rather than `input` as you did with synchronous custom validation (see Example 7-18).

Example 7-18. Revalidating on blur

```
form.elements.password.addEventListener('blur', async event => {
  const password = event.target;
  const errorElement = document.getElementById('password-error');
  if (password.dataset.shouldValidate) {
    await validatePasswordStrength(form);
    if (password.checkValidity()) {
      errorElement.textContent = '';
      password.classList.remove('border-danger');
    }
  }
});
```

Discussion

If you did this check on the `input` event, you'd be sending a network request every time the user pressed a key. The `blur` event defers the revalidation until the field loses focus. It calls the validation API again and checks the new validity state.

You could also use a debounced version of the validation function. This would revalidate on an input event, but only once the user has stopped typing for a certain period of time.

This article from freeCodeCamp (*https://oreil.ly/kLRJa*) goes into detail about how to create a debounced function. There are also npm packages available that will create a debounced version of a function.

CHAPTER 8

The Web Animations API

8.0 Introduction

There are a few different ways to animate elements in modern web browsers. Chapter 1 had an example of using the `requestAnimationFrame` API to manually animate an element (see Recipe 1.6). This gives you a lot of control, but at a cost. It requires keeping track of timestamps to calculate frame rates, and you must calculate each incremental change of the animation in JavaScript.

Keyframe-Based Animation

CSS3 introduced keyframe animations. You specify the beginning style, ending style, and a duration within CSS rules. The browser automatically interpolates, or fills in, the intermediate frames of the animation. Animations are defined with the `@key frames` rule and used via the `animation` property. Example 8-1 defines a fade-in animation.

Example 8-1. Using a CSS keyframe animation

```css
@keyframes fade {
  from {
    opacity: 0;
  }

  to {
    opacity: 1;
  }
}

.some-element {
```

```
  animation: fade 250ms;
}
```

A fade-in animation starts with an opacity of 0 and ends with an opacity of 1. When the animation runs, the browser calculates the intermediate style frames over the course of 250 milliseconds. The animation starts as soon as the element enters the DOM or the some-element class is applied.

Keyframe Animation with JavaScript

The Web Animations API lets you use keyframe animations in your JavaScript code. The Element interface has an animate method where you can define the keyframes and other options of the animation. Example 8-2 shows the same animation from Example 8-1 using the Web Animations API.

Example 8-2. Fading in with the Web Animations API

```
const element = document.querySelector('.some-element');
element.animate([
  { opacity: 0 },
  { opacity: 1 }
], {
  // Animate for 250 milliseconds
  duration: 250
});
```

The result is the same. The element fades in over the course of 250 milliseconds. In this case, the animation is triggered by the element.animate call.

Animation Objects

When you call element.animate, an Animation object is returned. This allows you to pause, resume, cancel, or even reverse an animation. It also provides you with a Promise that you can use to wait until the animation completes.

Be careful what properties you animate. Some properties, like height or padding, affect the layout of the rest of the page; animating them can cause performance issues, and the animations are usually not smooth. The best properties to animate are opacity and transform, as these don't affect the page layout and can even be accelerated by the system's GPU.

8.1 Applying a "Ripple" Effect on Click

Problem

You want to show a "ripple" animation when clicking a button, starting at the position within the button that the user clicked.

Solution

When the button is clicked, create a temporary child element for the "ripple". This is the element that will be animated.

First, create some styles for the ripple element. The button also needs a couple of styles applied (see Example 8-3).

Example 8-3. Styles for the button and ripple elements

```
.ripple-button {
  position: relative;
  overflow: hidden;
}

.ripple {
  background: white;
  pointer-events: none;
  transform-origin: center;
  opacity: 0;
  position: absolute;
  border-radius: 50%;
  width: 150px;
  height: 150px;
}
```

In the button's click handler, dynamically create a new ripple element and add it to the button, then update its position and perform the animation (see Example 8-4).

Example 8-4. Performing the ripple animation

```
button.addEventListener('click', async event => {
  // Create the temporary element for the ripple, set its class, and
  // add it to the button.
  const ripple = document.createElement('div');
  ripple.className = 'ripple';

  // Find the largest dimension (width or height) of the button and
  // use that as the ripple's size.
  const rippleSize = Math.max(button.offsetWidth, button.offsetHeight);
  ripple.style.width = `${rippleSize}px`;
```

```
    ripple.style.height = `${rippleSize}px`;

    // Center the ripple element on the click location.
    ripple.style.top = `${event.offsetY - (rippleSize / 2)}px`;
    ripple.style.left = `${event.offsetX - (rippleSize / 2)}px`;

    button.appendChild(ripple);

    // Perform the ripple animation and wait for it to complete.
    await ripple.animate([
      { transform: 'scale(0)', opacity: 0.5 },
      { transform: 'scale(2.5)', opacity: 0 }
    ], {
      // Animate for 500 milliseconds.
      duration: 500,
      // Use the ease-in easing function.
      easing: 'ease-in'
    }).finished;

    // All done, remove the ripple element.
    ripple.remove();
});
```

Discussion

The ripple element is a circle, sized relative to the size of the button. You achieve the ripple effect by animating its opacity and scale transform.

There are a few things here to point out about the element styles. First, the button itself has its position set to relative. This is so that when you set the ripple's absolute position, it is relative to the button itself.

CSS Absolute Positioning

When you set an element's position property to absolute, the browser removes it from the document layout and positions it relative to its nearest ancestor element that is *positioned*. An element is considered positioned if it has a position property set to anything but the default of static.

If you have an element with absolute positioning, and the position doesn't seem right, check to make sure that it's using the correct positioned ancestor. This may or may not be the element's immediate parent.

The button also has overflow: hidden. This prevents the ripple effect from being visible outside of the button.

You may also notice that the ripple has pointer-events: none set. Because the ripple is inside the button, the browser delegates any click events on the ripple up to the button. This means clicking the ripple triggers a new ripple, but the position is wrong because it's based on the click position within the ripple rather than within the button.

The easiest way to get around this is to set `pointer-events: none`, which makes the ripple element ignore click events. If you click on a ripple while it is animating, the click event goes to the button, which is what you want in order to have the next ripple be positioned properly.

Next, the ripple code sets the top and left position such that the center of the ripple is where you just clicked.

Then the ripple is animated. The animation returned by `ripple.animate` has a `finished` property, which is a `Promise` that you can wait for. Once this `Promise` resolves, the ripple animation is complete and you can remove the element from the DOM.

If you click the button while a ripple is in progress, another ripple starts and they'll animate together—the first animation isn't interrupted. This is more difficult to achieve with regular CSS animations.

Easing Functions

An easing function, specified by the `easing` property, defines the rate of change of the properties being animated. Customizing and fine-tuning these are beyond the scope of this book, but there are a few built-in ones to understand:

`linear` *(the default)*
> The animation happens at a constant rate.

`ease-out`
> The animation starts faster, then gradually slows down.

`ease-in`
> The animation starts slow, then gradually speeds up.

`ease-in-out`
> The animation starts slow, speeds up, then slows down again at the end.

8.2 Starting and Stopping Animations

Problem

You want to be able to programmatically start or stop an animation.

Solution

Use the animation's pause and play functions (see Example 8-5).

Example 8-5. Toggling an animation's play state

```
/**
 * Given an animation, toggles the animation state.
 * If the animation is running, it will be paused.
 * If it is paused, it will be resumed.
 */
function toggleAnimation(animation) {
  if (animation.playState === 'running') {
    animation.pause();
  } else {
    animation.play();
  }
}
```

Discussion

The Animation object returned from an element.animate call has a playState property, which you can use to determine if the animation is currently running or not. If it is running, its value is the string running. Other values are:

paused
    The animation was running, but was stopped before it finished.

finished
    The animation ran to completion and stopped.

Depending on the playState property, the toggleAnimation function calls either pause or play to set the desired animation state.

8.3 Animating DOM Insertion and Removal

Problem

You want to add to, or remove elements from, the DOM with an animation effect.

Solution

The solution differs slightly for each operation.

For *adding* an element, add the element to the DOM first then immediately run the animation (such as a fade in). Since only elements in the DOM can be animated, you need to add it before running the animation (see Example 8-6).

Example 8-6. Showing an element with an animation

```
/**
 * Shows an element that was just added to the DOM with a fade-in animation.
 * @param element The element to show
 */
function showElement(element) {
  document.body.appendChild(element);
  element.animate([
    { opacity: 0 },
    { opacity: 1 }
  ], {
    // Animate for 250 milliseconds.
    duration: 250
  });
}
```

To *remove* an element, you need to run the animation *first* (such as a fade out). Once the animation completes, immediately remove the element from the DOM (see Example 8-7).

Example 8-7. Removing an element with an animation

```
/**
 * Removes an element from the DOM after performing a fade-out animation.
 * @param element The element to remove
 */
async function removeElement(element) {
  // First, perform the animation and make the element disappear from view.
  // The resulting animation's 'finished' property is a Promise.
  await element.animate([
    { opacity: 1 },
    { opacity: 0 }
  ], {
    // Animate for 250 milliseconds.
    duration: 250
  }).finished;

  // Animation is done, now remove the element from the DOM.
  element.remove();
}
```

Discussion

When you run the animation at the same time you add the element, it begins animating from zero opacity before it has a chance to initially be rendered. This produces the effect you want—an element that is hidden and fades into view.

When you're removing the element, you can use the animation's finished Promise to wait until the animation is finished. You don't want to remove the element from the

DOM until the animation is completely finished, otherwise the effect could only run partially and the element would disappear.

8.4 Reversing Animations

Problem

You want to cancel an in-progress animation, such as a hover effect, and smoothly revert it back to the initial state.

Solution

Use the `Animation` object's `reverse` method to start playing in the reverse direction.

You can keep track of the in-progress animation with a variable. When you change the desired animation state, and this variable has a value, it means another animation is already in progress and the browser should reverse it.

In the example of a hover effect (see Example 8-8), you can start the animation when the mouse hovers over the element.

Example 8-8. The hover effect

```
element.addEventListener('mouseover', async () => {
  if (animation) {
    // There was already an animation in progress. Instead of starting a new
    // animation, reverse the current one.
    animation.reverse();
  } else {
    // Nothing is in progress, so start a new animation.
    animation = element.animate([
      { transform: 'scale(1)' },
      { transform: 'scale(2)' }
    ], {
      // Animate for 1 second.
      duration: 1000,
      // Apply the initial and end styles.
      fill: 'both'
    });

    // Once the animation finishes, set the current animation to null.
    await animation.finished;
    animation = null;
  }
});
```

When the mouse moves away, the same logic applies (see Example 8-9).

Example 8-9. Removing the hover effect

```
button.addEventListener('mouseout', async () => {
  if (animation) {
    // There was already an animation in progress. Instead of starting a new
    // animation, reverse the current one.
    animation.reverse();
  } else {
    // Nothing is in progress, so start a new animation.
    animation = button.animate([
      { transform: 'scale(2)' },
      { transform: 'scale(1)' }
    ], {
      // Animate for 1 second.
      duration: 1000,
      // Apply the initial and end styles.
      fill: 'both'
    });

    // Once the animation finishes, set the current animation to null.
    await animation.finished;
    animation = null;
  }
});
```

Discussion

Since the keyframes are the same in each case (they only differ in their order), you can have a single animation function that sets the animation's direction property. When the mouse hovers over the element, you want to run the element in the for ward, or normal, direction. When the mouse leaves, you'll run the same animation, but with the direction set to reverse (see Example 8-10).

Example 8-10. A single animation function

```
async function animate(element, direction) {
  if (animation) {
    animation.reverse();
  } else {
    animation = element.animate([
      { transform: 'scale(1)' },
      { transform: 'scale(2)' }
    ], {
      // Animate for 1 second.
      duration: 1000,
      // Apply the end style after the animation is done.
      fill: 'forward',
      // Run the animation forward (normal) or backward (reverse)
      // depending on the direction argument.
      direction
```

```
  });

  // Once the animation finishes, set the variable to
  // null to signal that there is no animation in progress.
  await animation.finished;
  animation = null;
  }
}

element.addEventListener('mouseover', () => {
  animate(element, 'normal');
});

element.addEventListener('mouseout', () => {
  animate(element, 'reverse');
});
```

The result is the same as before. When you hover over the element, it starts to increase in size due to the scale(2) transform. If you move the mouse away, it starts shrinking again by reversing the animation's direction.

The difference is in the event handlers. They both call a single function, using different values for the animation's direction option.

Example 8-8 sets the animation's *fill* mode to both. The animation's fill mode determines the style of the element before and after the animation. By default, the fill mode is none. This means that when the animation completes, the element's style jumps back to what it was before the animation.

In practice, this means that when you hover over the element, it starts growing until it reaches its final size, but then it immediately jumps back to its original size, due to no fill mode being set.

There are three options (other than none) for the fill mode:

backward
    The element's style is set to the animation's starting keyframe before the animation starts. This is usually only applicable when using an animation delay, as it defines what the element's style is within the delay period.

forward
    After the animation finishes, the ending keyframe styles remain applied.

both
    Applies the rules of both backward and forward.

The animation in Example 8-10 has no delay, so the forward option is used to retain the style after the animation ends.

8.5 Showing a Scroll Progress Indicator

Problem

You want to show a bar at the top of the page that moves as you scroll. As you scroll down, the bar moves to the right.

Solution

Use a scroll-linked animation by creating a `ScrollTimeline` and passing it to the element's `animate` method. To make the element grow from left to right, you can animate the `transition` property from `scaleX(0)` to `scaleX(1)`.

 This API may not be supported by all browsers yet. See CanIUse (*https://oreil.ly/l-hvN*) for the latest compatibility data.

First, set some styles for the progress bar element, as shown in Example 8-11.

Example 8-11. Scroll progress bar styles

```css
.scroll-progress {
  height: 8px;
  transform-origin: left;
  position: sticky;
  top: 0;
  transform: scaleX(0);
  background: blue;
}
```

The `position: sticky` property ensures that the element remains visible as you scroll down the page. Also, its initial style is set to `scaleX(0)`, which effectively hides it. Without this, the bar would appear at its full width for an instant then disappear. This ensures you won't see the bar at all until you scroll.

Next, create a `ScrollTimeline` object and pass it as the animation's `timeline` option, as shown in Example 8-12.

Example 8-12. Creating the scroll timeline

```js
const progress = document.querySelector('.scroll-progress');

// Create a timeline that's linked to the document's
// scroll position.
```

```
const timeline = new ScrollTimeline({
  source: document.documentElement
});

// Start the animation, passing the timeline you just created.
progress.animate(
  [
    { transform: 'scaleX(0)' },
    { transform: 'scaleX(1)' }
  ],
  { timeline });
```

You now have a scroll-linked animation.

Discussion

An animation's *timeline* is an object that implements the `AnimationTimeline` interface. By default, an animation uses the document's default timeline, which is a `DocumentTimeline` object. This is a timeline that's linked to elapsed time on the clock. When you start an animation with the default timeline, it starts at the initial keyframe and runs forward until it reaches the end (or you stop it manually). Because this type of timeline is linked to elapsed time, it has a defined start value and continuously increases as time passes.

However, a *scroll-linked* animation provides a timeline linked to the scroll position. When you scroll all the way to the top, the scroll position is 0 and the animation remains at its initial state. As you scroll down, the position increases and the animation advances. Once you have scrolled all the way to the bottom, the animation reaches its end. If you scroll back up, the animation runs in reverse.

A `ScrollTimeline` is given a source element. In Example 8-12, the source is the document element (the body tag). You can pass any scrollable element as the source, and the `ScrollTimeline` uses that element's scroll position to determine the current progress.

At the time of writing, `DocumentTimeline` is supported in all modern browsers but `ScrollTimeline` is not. Be sure to always check browser support before using a `ScrollTimeline`.

8.6 Making an Element Bounce

Problem

You want to apply a momentary bouncing effect to an element.

Solution

Apply a series of animations, one after another. Use an animation's `finished` `Promise` to wait for it to finish before running the next one.

The element moves up and down three times. On each pass, the element is moved up the page by applying a `translateY` transform, then back down to its original position. The first pass bounces the element by 40 pixels, the second by 20 pixels, and the third by 10 pixels. This gives the appearance of gravity slowing the bounce down each time. This can be done with a `for-of` loop (see Example 8-13).

Example 8-13. Applying the bounce animations in series

```
async function animateBounce(element) {
  const distances = [ '40px', '20px', '10px' ];
  for (let distance of distances) {
    // Wait for this animation to complete before continuing.
    await element.animate([
      // Start at the bottom.
      { transform: 'translateY(0)' },

      // Move up by the current distance.
      { transform: `translateY(-${distance})`, offset: 0.5 },

      // Back to the bottom
      { transform: 'translateY(0)' }
    ], {
      // Animate for 250 milliseconds.
      duration: 250,

      // Use a more fluid easing function than linear
      // (the default).
      easing: 'ease-in-out'
    }).finished;
  }
}
```

Discussion

This example demonstrates an advantage of the Web Animations API: dynamic key-frame values. Each iteration through the loop uses a different `distance` value inside the keyframe effect.

The `for-of` loop walks through the three distances (40px, 20px, and 10px) and animates them in turn. In each iteration, it moves the element up by the given distance and back down again. The key is the last line, where it references the animation's `finished` property. This ensures that the next loop iteration doesn't start until the current animation finishes. The result is the animations run in series, one after the other, providing the bounce effect.

You may be wondering why this example uses a for-of loop rather than a forEach() call on the array. Using await inside array methods such as forEach does not work as you'd expect. These methods were not designed for asynchronous use. If you used a forEach call, the element.animate calls would all be called immediately after one another, resulting in only the last animation being played. Using a for-of loop (a regular for loop would work as well) works as expected with async/await and gives the desired result.

8.7 Running Multiple Animations Simultaneously

Problem

You want to apply multiple transforms to an element using multiple animations.

Solution

Call animate on the element multiple times, with the different transform keyframes. You must also specify the composite property to combine the transforms, as shown in Example 8-14.

Example 8-14. Combining two transform animations

```
// The first animation will move the element back and forth on the x-axis.
element.animate([
  { transform: 'translateX(0)' },
  { transform: 'translateX(250px)' }
], {
  // Animate for 5 seconds.
  duration: 5000,
  // Run the animation forward, then run it in reverse.
  direction: 'alternate',
  // Repeat the animation forever.
  iterations: Infinity,
  // Slow to start, fast in the middle, slow at the end.
  easing: 'ease-in-out'
});

// The second animation rotates the element.
element.animate([
  { transform: 'rotate(0deg)' },
  { transform: 'rotate(360deg)' }
], {
  // Animate for 3 seconds.
  duration: 3000,
```

```
  // Repeat the animation forever.
  iterations: Infinity,
  // Combine the effects with other running animations.
  composite: 'add'
});
```

The `alternate` direction means the animation runs forward to completion, then runs backward to completion. Because `iterations` is set to `Infinity`, the animation runs forever.

Discussion

The key to this effect is the `composite` property added to the second animation. If you don't specify `composite: add`, you *only* see the `rotate` transform because it overrides the `translateX` transform. The element would rotate but not move horizontally.

This, in effect, combines both transforms into a single transform. Also note, however, that these transforms are happening at different rates. The rotation lasts for three seconds, while the translation lasts for five. The animations use different easing functions as well. Despite the different options, the browser smoothly combines the animations.

8.8 Showing a Loading Animation

Problem

You want to show a loading indicator to the user while waiting for a network request to complete.

Solution

Create and style the loading indicator, then apply an infinite rotation animation to it until the `Promise` returned by `fetch` resolves.

To make a smooth effect, you can first apply a fade-in animation. Once the `Promise` resolves, you can fade it out.

First, create a loader element and define some styles, as shown in Example 8-15.

Example 8-15. The loader element

```
<style>
  #loader {
    width: 64px;
    height: 64px;

    /* Make a circle shape */
```

```
    border-radius: 50%;
    border-width: 10px;
    border-style: solid;
    border-color: skyblue blue skyblue blue;

    /* Set the initial opacity so the animation that appears is smooth */
    opacity: 0;
  }
</style>

<div id="loader"></div>
```

The loader is a ring with alternating border colors, as shown in Figure 8-1.

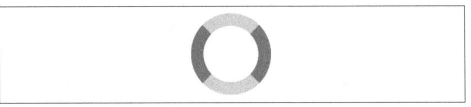

Figure 8-1. The styled loader

Next, define a function that starts the animation and wait for the Promise, as shown in Example 8-16.

Example 8-16. The loader animations

```
async function showLoader(promise) {
  const loader = document.querySelector('#loader');

  // Start the spin animation before fading in.
  const spin = loader.animate([
    { transform: 'rotate(0deg)' },
    { transform: 'rotate(360deg)' }
  ], { duration: 1000, iterations: Infinity });

  // Since the opacity is 0, the loader isn't visible yet.
  // Show it with a fade-in animation.
  // The loader will continue spinning as it fades in.
  loader.animate([
    { opacity: 0 },
    { opacity: 1 }
  ], { duration: 500, fill: 'both' });

  // Wait for the Promise to resolve.
  await promise;

  // The Promise is done. Now fade the loader out.
  // Don't stop the spin animation until the fade out is complete.
```

```
// You can wait by awaiting the 'finished' Promise.
await loader.animate([
  { opacity: 1 },
  { opacity: 0 }
], { duration: 500, fill: 'both' }).finished;

// Finally, stop the spin animation.
spin.cancel();

// Return the original Promise to allow chaining.
return promise;
}
```

You can now pass your `fetch` call as an argument to `showLoader`, as shown in Example 8-17.

Example 8-17. Using the loader

```
showLoader(
  fetch('https://example.com/api/users')
    .then(response => response.json())
);
```

Discussion

You don't necessarily need the Web Animations API to create an animated loader—you can do that with plain CSS. As this example shows, though, the Web Animations API lets you combine multiple animations. The infinite spin animation continues to run while the fade-in animation runs. This is a little tricky to do with regular CSS animations.

8.9 Respecting the User's Animation Preference

Problem

You want to tone down, or disable, animations if the user has configured their operating system to reduce motion.

Solution

Use `window.matchMedia` to check the `prefers-reduced-motion` media query (see Example 8-18).

Example 8-18. Using the prefers-reduced-motion media query

```
if (!window.matchMedia('(prefers-reduced-motion: reduce)').matches) {
  // Reduced motion is not enabled, so animate normally.
```

```
} else {
  // Skip this animation or run a less intense one.
}
```

Discussion

This is extremely important for accessibility. Users with epilepsy or vestibular disorders could have seizures, migraines, or other ill effects triggered by a large or fast-moving animation.

You don't necessarily have to disable animation altogether; you could instead use a more subtle one. Suppose you are showing an element with a bounce effect that looks really good but could be disorienting for some users. If the user has reduced motion enabled, you could instead provide a simple fade-in animation.

CHAPTER 9

The Web Speech API

9.0 Introduction

In the age of smart devices and assistants, your voice has become another commonly used input method. Whether you're dictating a text message or asking for tomorrow's weather forecast, speech recognition and synthesis are becoming useful tools in app development. With the Web Speech API, you can make your app speak or listen for a user's voice input.

Speech Recognition

The Web Speech API brings speech *recognition* to the browser. Once the user gives you permission to use the microphone, it listens for speech. When it recognizes a series of words, it triggers an event with the recognized content.

 Speech recognition may not be supported by all browsers yet. See CanIUse (*https://oreil.ly/SGLlc*) for the latest compatibility data.

You'll need the user's permission before you can start listening for speech. Due to privacy settings, the first time you attempt to listen, the user is prompted to grant your app permission to use the microphone (see Figure 9-1).

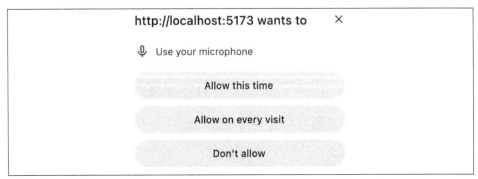

Figure 9-1. A microphone permission request in Chrome

Some browsers, such as Chrome, use an external server for analyzing the captured audio to recognize speech. This means speech recognition won't work when you're offline, and it might also raise privacy concerns.

Speech Recognition Versus Language Processing

It's important to distinguish between speech recognition (determining what words were spoken) and language processing (understanding what those words mean). The Web Speech API, on its own, does not give any meaning to the recognized words; it returns them to you as a string and it's up to you to do any additional processing. You can integrate this data with third-party natural language processing (NLP) APIs such as Microsoft LUIS or IBM Watson NLP. These APIs and services are beyond the scope of this book.

Speech Synthesis

The Web Speech API also provides speech *synthesis*. Given some text, it can create a synthesized voice that speaks the text. The browser has a set of built-in voices that it can use to speak your content. Once you have selected a voice appropriate for the target language, you can customize the voice's pitch and speaking rate.

You can combine speech recognition and synthesis to create conversational voice user interfaces. They can listen for a question or command and speak the output or feedback.

Browser Support

At the time of writing, support for the Web Speech API is somewhat limited.

The specification for this API also adds a few other pieces that enhance speech recognition and synthesis once they are supported in browsers.

The first of these is custom grammar, which lets you fine-tune speech recognition by specifying words and phrases that you want to recognize. For example, if you were designing a calculator with voice commands, your custom grammar would include digits ("one," "two," etc.) and calculator operations ("plus," "minus," etc.). Using a custom grammar helps guide the speech recognition engine to capture the words your application is looking for.

The SpeechSynthesis API supports Speech Synthesis Markup Language (SSML). SSML is an XML language that customizes speech synthesis. You can switch between male and female voices or specify that the browser should read something letter by letter. At the time of writing, SSML markup is parsed and understood—the engine won't speak the markup tags—but browsers currently ignore most instructions.

9.1 Adding Dictation to a Text Field

Problem

You want to recognize spoken text and add it to a text field's content, allowing the user to dictate the text field's contents.

Solution

Use the `SpeechRecognition` interface to listen for speech. When speech is recognized, extract the recognized text and append it to the text field (see Example 9-1).

Example 9-1. Adding basic dictation to a text field

```
/**
 * Starts listening for speech. When speech is recognized, it is appended
 * to the given text field's value.
 * Recognition continues until the returned recognition object is stopped.
 *
 * @param textField A text field to append to
 * @returns The recognition object
 */
function startDictation(textField) {
  // Only proceed if this browser supports speech recognition.
  if ('webkitSpeechRecognition' in window || 'SpeechRecognition' in window) {
    const SpeechRecognition = window.SpeechRecognition
    || window.webkitSpeechRecognition;
    const recognition = new SpeechRecognition();
    recognition.continuous = true;

    recognition.addEventListener('result', event => {
      const result = event.results[event.resultIndex];
      textField.value += result[0].transcript;
    });
```

```
  recognition.addEventListener('error', event => {
    console.log('error', event);
  });

  recognition.start();

  // Return the recognition object so recognition
  // can be stopped later (like when the user clicks a toggle button).
  return recognition;
  }
}
```

Discussion

At the time of writing, in the WebKit browsers that support it, the SpeechRecogni
tion constructor is prefixed as webkitSpeechRecognition. In unsupported browsers,
neither SpeechRecognition nor webkitSpeechRecognition are defined, so it's
important to check the browser support before continuing.

To future-proof the code, the example checks for either the prefixed version (webkit
SpeechRecognition) as well as the standard SpeechRecognition version. This way,
you won't have to change the code to accommodate browsers that implement the API
in the future.

Next, the startDictation function creates a SpeechRecognition object and sets its
continuous flag to true. By default, no further recognition is performed once a result
is recognized. Setting the continuous flag tells the speech recognition engine to continue listening and to deliver additional results.

When the recognition engine recognizes some speech, it triggers a result event. This
event has a results property that is an array-like object (actually a SpeechRecogni
tionResultList object) containing the results.

When operating in continuous mode, as this example does, the results list contains
all results that the recognition engine recognized. The first time the user speaks and
some speech is recognized, this has a single result. When the user speaks again and
the browser recognizes some more words, there are *two* results—the original result
and the new one that was just recognized. If you set continuous to false (the
default), the engine only recognizes one phrase, then no further result events are
triggered.

Helpfully, the event also has a resultIndex property that points to the index within
the list of the new result that triggered this event.

The result object is another array-like object (a SpeechRecognitionAlternative
object). When you create a SpeechRecognition object, you can give it the property

---

maxAlternatives. The browser presents a list of possible matches for the recognized speech, each with a confidence value. However, the default maxAlternatives value is 1, so this dictation code only ever has one SpeechRecognitionAlternative object in the list.

Finally, this object has a transcript property that is the actual phrase that the engine recognized. You can take this value and append it to the text field's current value.

Calling start on the recognition object begins listening for speech, emitting events when it hears something. The startDictation function then returns the recognition object, so that you can stop recognition once the user is finished dictating.

Like with any API, it's also important to handle any errors that occur. With speech recognition, some common errors you might face are:

Permission error
> If the user did not grant permission to use the microphone. The event has an error property of not-allowed.

Network error
> If the browser couldn't reach the speech recognition service. This has an error of network.

Hardware error
> If the browser was unable to access the microphone. This has an error code of audio-capture.

9.2 Creating a Promise Helper for Speech Recognition

Problem

You want to encapsulate speech recognition into a single function call.

Solution

Wrap the speech recognition call in a new Promise inside a helper function. Within the helper function, create a new SpeechRecognition object and listen for speech. You can resolve the Promise when the browser recognizes some speech (see Example 9-2).

Example 9-2. A Promise helper for speech recognition

```
/**
 * Listens for speech and performs speech recognition.
 * Assumes that speech recognition is available in the current browser.
 * @returns a Promise that is resolved with the recognized transcript when speech
```

```
 * is recognized, and rejects on an error.
 */
function captureSpeech() {
  const speechPromise = new Promise((resolve, reject) => {
    const SpeechRecognition = window.SpeechRecognition ||
      window.webkitSpeechRecognition;

    // If this browser doesn't support speech recognition, reject the Promise.
    if (!SpeechRecognition) {
      reject('Speech recognition is not supported on this browser.')
    }

    const recognition = new SpeechRecognition();

    // Resolve the promise on successful speech recognition.
    recognition.addEventListener('result', event => {
      const result = event.results[event.resultIndex];
      resolve(result[0].transcript);
    });

    recognition.addEventListener('error', event => {
      // Reject the promise if there was a recognition error.
      reject(event);
    });

    // Start listening for speech.
    recognition.start();
  });

  // Whether there was successful speech recognition or an error, make sure
  // the recognition engine has stopped listening.
  return speechPromise.finally(() => {
    recognition.stop();
  });
}
```

Discussion

The captureSpeech helper does not use continuous mode. This means you can only use it to listen for a single speech recognition event. If you want to capture additional speech after the returned Promise resolves, you need to call captureSpeech again and wait on the new Promise.

You might notice that Example 9-2 doesn't return the Promise directly. Instead, it calls finally on that Promise to stop the speech recognition engine regardless of the outcome. The captureSpeech function lets you quickly recognize speech by just waiting on a Promise (see Example 9-3).

Example 9-3. Using the captureSpeech helper

```
const spokenText = await captureSpeech();
```

9.3 Getting the Available Voices

Problem

You want to determine what speech synthesis voices are available in the current browser.

Solution

Query the voice list by calling `speechSynthesis.getVoices`, and then listen for the `voiceschanged` event if necessary, as shown in Example 9-4.

Example 9-4. Getting the list of available speech synthesis voices

```
function showVoices() {
  speechSynthesis.getVoices().forEach(voice => {
    console.log('Voice:', voice.name);
  });
}

// Some browsers load the voice list asynchronously. In these browsers,
// the voices are available when the voiceschanged event is triggered.
speechSynthesis.addEventListener('voiceschanged', () => showVoices());

// Show the voices immediately in those browsers that support it.
showVoices();
```

Discussion

Some browsers, such as Chrome, load the list of voices asynchronously. If you call `getVoices` before the list is ready, you'll get an empty array back. The `speechSynthesis` object triggers a `voiceschanged` event when the list is ready.

Other browsers, including Firefox, have the voice list available right away. In these browsers, the `voiceschanged` event never fires. The code in Example 9-4 handles both cases.

Each voice has a `lang` property that specifies the voice's language. When speaking text, the voice uses the pronunciation rules for its language. Make sure you use a voice with the correct language for the text you're synthesizing. Otherwise, the pronunciation won't sound right.

9.4 Synthesizing Speech

Problem

You want your app to speak some text to the user.

Solution

Create a `SpeechSynthesisUtterance` and pass it to the `speechSynthesis.speak` method (see Example 9-5).

Example 9-5. Speaking some text with the Web Speech API

```
function speakText(text) {
  const utterance = new SpeechSynthesisUtterance(text);
  speechSynthesis.speak(utterance);
}
```

Discussion

An utterance is the set of words you want the browser to speak. It's created with a `SpeechSynthesisUtterance` object.

 Browsers will only permit speech synthesis once the user has interacted with the page in some way. This is to stop a page from speaking immediately upon loading. As such, the `speakText` helper function will not speak anything until there is some user activity on the page.

This speaks the text with the default voice. If you want to use a different supported system voice, you can use the technique from Recipe 9.3 to get the array of available voices. You can set the utterance's `voice` property to one of the voice objects from this array, as shown in Example 9-6.

Example 9-6. Using another voice

```
// Assuming the voices are available now
const aliceVoice = speechSynthesis
  .getVoices()
  .find(voice => voice.name === 'Alice');

function speakText(text) {
  const utterance = new SpeechSynthesisUtterance(text);

  // Make sure the "Alice" voice was found.
  if (aliceVoice) {
```

```
    utterance.voice = aliceVoice;
  }

  speechSynthesis.speak(utterance);
}
```

9.5 Customizing Speech Synthesis Parameters

Problem

You want to speed up, slow down, or adjust the pitch of the spoken text.

Solution

When creating a `SpeechSynthesisUtterance`, use the `rate` and `pitch` properties to customize the speaking voice (see Example 9-7).

Example 9-7. Customizing speech output

```
const utteranceLow =
new SpeechSynthesisUtterance('This is spoken slowly in a low tone');
utterance.pitch = 0.1;
utterance.rate = 0.5;
speechSynthesis.speak(utterance);

const utteranceHigh =
new SpeechSynthesisUtterance('This is spoken quickly in a high tone');
utterance.pitch = 2;
utterance.rate = 2;
speechSynthesis.speak(utterance);
```

Discussion

The `pitch` option is a float number that can have a value between 0 and 2. Lower values result in a lower pitch, and higher values result in a higher pitch. Lowering the pitch does not affect the speaking rate. Depending on the browser or voice being used, the range of supported pitch values may be limited.

To speed up or slow down the speaking rate, you can adjust the `rate` property. Each voice has a default speaking rate, which is represented by a `rate` of 1. The value of `rate` has a multiplier effect. If you set `rate` to 0.5, it is half of the default speaking rate. Similarly, if you set `rate` to 1.5, it is 50% faster than the default rate. The specification defines the valid range as 0.1 to 10, but browsers and voices typically limit this to a smaller range.

9.6 Automatically Pausing Speech

Problem

When your app is speaking, you want to pause speech when you switch to another tab so that it doesn't interfere with the usage of the other tab. You also want to stop speaking when leaving the page.

Solution

Listen for the `visibilitychange` event and check the `document.visibilityState` property. When the page becomes hidden, pause speech synthesis. When it becomes visible again, resume speaking (see Example 9-8).

Example 9-8. Pausing speech when the page becomes hidden

```
document.addEventListener('visibilitychange', () => {
  // speechSynthesis.speaking is true:
  // (1) when speech is currently being spoken
  // (2) when speech was being spoken, but is paused
  if (speechSynthesis.speaking) {
    if (document.visibilityState === 'hidden') {
      speechSynthesis.pause();
    } else if (document.visibilityState === 'visible') {
      speechSynthesis.resume();
    }
  }
});
```

Discussion

By default, if you switch to another tab while the Web Speech API is speaking some text, it continues speaking. This might be what you expect—after all, the same thing happens if you are streaming audio or video then change to another tab; you'll continue to hear the audio from the other tab.

When you switch tabs, the `visibilitychange` event fires. The event itself doesn't have any information about the visibility state, but you can get that by checking the `document.visibilityState` property. Example 9-8 pauses the speech when you switch to another tab. When you switch back, it continues where it left off.

Some browsers keep playing the speech even when you navigate away from the page or perform a full page refresh. Leaving or refreshing the page also triggers the `visibilitychange` event, so the code in Example 9-8 correctly stops the speech in these cases as well.

CHAPTER 10

Working with Files

10.0 Introduction

Reading and writing files are part of many applications. In the past, you couldn't really work with local files within the browser. To read data, you'd upload a file to a backend server, which would process it and return data to the browser.

To write data, the server would send a downloadable file. Without browser plug-ins, there wasn't a way to work directly with files.

Today, browsers have first-class support for reading and writing files. The `file` input type opens a file chooser and provides data about the selected file. You can also limit the supported files to specific extensions or MIME types. From there, the File API can read the contents of the file into memory.

Taking it a step further, the File System API enables your JavaScript code to interact directly with the local filesystem, without needing a file input to select a file first (though, depending on settings, the user may need to grant permission!).

You can use these APIs to create text editors, image viewers, audio or video players, and more.

10.1 Loading Text from a File

Problem

You want to load some text data from the user's local filesystem.

Solution

Use an `<input type="file">` to select the file (see Example 10-1).

Example 10-1. A file input

```
<input type="file" id="select-file">
```

When you click on the file input, the browser will show a dialog where you can browse files and folders on the local system. The exact dialog shown will depend on the browser and operating system version. Navigate to, and select, the desired file. One you have a selected file, use a `FileReader` as shown in Example 10-2 to read the file's text content.

Example 10-2. Loading plain text from a file

```
/**
 * Reads the text content of a file.
 * @param file The File object containing the data to be read
 * @param onSuccess A function to call when the data is available
 */
function readFileContent(file, onSuccess) {
  const reader = new FileReader();

  // When the content is loaded, the reader will emit a
  // 'load' event.
  reader.addEventListener('load', event => {
    onSuccess(event.target.result);
  });

  // Always handle errors!
  reader.addEventListener('error', event => {
    console.error('Error reading file:', event);
  });

  // Start the file read operation.
  reader.readAsText(file);
}

const fileInput = document.querySelector('#select-file');

// The input fires a 'change' event when a file is selected.
fileInput.addEventListener('change', event => {
  // This is an array, because a file input can be used to select
  // multiple files. Here, there's only once file selected.
  // This is using array destructuring syntax to get the first file.
  const [file] = fileInput.files;

  readFileContent(file, content => {
    // The file's text content is now available.
    // Imagine you have a textarea element you want to set the text in.
    const textArea = document.querySelector('.file-content-textarea');
    textArea.textContent = content;
```

```
    });
});
```

Discussion

A FileReader is an object that reads files asynchronously. It can read a file's content in several different ways, depending on the type of file. Example 10-2 uses the readAs Text method, which retrieves the file content as plain text.

If you have a binary file, such as a ZIP archive or image, you can use readAsBinary String. An image can be read as a data URL with Base64-encoded image data using readAsDataURL, which you'll see in Recipe 10.2.

This API is event based, so the readFileContent function takes a callback function that is called with the content when it's ready.

You could also wrap this with a Promise to make a Promise-based API, as shown in Example 10-3.

Example 10-3. Promisified readFileContent function

```
function readFileContent(file) {
  const reader = new FileReader();

  return new Promise((resolve, reject) => {
    reader.addEventListener('load', event => {
      resolve(event.target.result);
    });

    reader.addEventListener('error', reject);

    reader.readAsText(file);
  });
}

try {
  const content = await readFileContent(inputFile);
  const textArea = document.querySelector('.file-content-textarea');
  textArea.textContent = content;
} catch (error) {
  console.error('Error reading file content:', error);
}
```

Once you have the text content, you can add it to the page in several ways. You could set it as the textContent of a DOM node, or you could even load it into a textarea to make the content editable.

10.2 Loading an Image as a Data URL

Problem

You want to let the user select a local image file, then display that image on the page.

Solution

Use the `readAsDataURL` method of `FileReader` to get a Base64-encoded data URL, then set that as the `src` attribute of an `img` tag (see Examples 10-4 and 10-5).

Example 10-4. File input and image placeholder

```
<input
  type="file"
  id="select-file"
  accept="image/*"  ❶
>
<img id="placeholder-image">
```

❶ Restricts the file chooser to only allow images to be selected. A wildcard pattern is used here, but you can also specify an exact MIME type such as `image/png`.

Example 10-5. Loading an image into the page

```
/**
 * Loads and shows an image from a file.
 * @param file The File object containing the image data
 * @param imageElement A placeholder Image element that will
 *                      show the image data
 */
function showImageFile(file, imageElement) {
  const reader = new FileReader();

  reader.addEventListener('load', event => {
    // Set the data URL directly as the image's
    // src attribute to load the image.
    imageElement.src = event.target.result;
  });

  reader.addEventListener('error', event => {
    console.log('error', event);
  });

  reader.readAsDataURL(file);
}

const fileInput = document.querySelector('#select-file');
```

```
fileInput.addEventListener('change', event => {
  showImageFile(
    fileInput.files[0],
    document.querySelector('#placeholder-image')
  );
});
```

Discussion

A data URL has the `data` URL scheme. It specifies the data's MIME type, then the image data is included in Base64-encoded format:

```
data:image/png;base64,UHJldGVuZCB0aGlzIGlzIGltYWdlIGRhdGE=
```

When the `FileReader` returns the image encoded as a data URL, the data URL is set as the image element's `src` attribute. This renders the image in the page.

It's important to note that this is all being done locally in the user's browser. Nothing is being uploaded to a remote server, as the File API works on the local filesystem.

Recipe 4.4 in Chapter 4 shows an example of using an `<input type="file">` to upload file data to a remote server, though this uses the FormData API instead of the File API.

For more details about data URLs and Base64 encoding, see this article from MDN (*https://oreil.ly/kMtDy*).

10.3 Loading a Video as an Object URL

Problem

You want the user to select a video file, then play it in the browser.

Solution

Create an object URL for the `File` object, and set it as the `src` attribute of a `<video>` element.

First, you'll need a `<video>` element and an `<input type="file">` to select the video file (see Example 10-6).

Example 10-6. The video player markup

```
<input
  id="file-upload"
  type="file"
  accept="video/*" ❶
>
```

```
<video
  id="video-player"
  controls ❷
>
```

❶ Only allows the selection of video files

❷ Tells the browser to include playback controls

Next, listen for the file input's `change` event and create an object URL, as shown in Example 10-7.

Example 10-7. Playing the video file

```
const fileInput = document.querySelector('#file-upload');
const video = document.querySelector('#video-player');

fileInput.addEventListener('change', event => {
  const [file] = fileInput.files;

  // File extends from Blob, which can be passed to
  // createObjectURL.
  const objectUrl = URL.createObjectURL(file);

  // The <video> element can take the object URL to load the video.
  video.src = objectUrl;
});
```

Discussion

An object URL is a special URL that refers to the file content. You can do this without a `FileReader`, since the file itself has a `createObjectURL` method. This URL can be passed to the <video> element.

Data URLs and Object URLs

There are some important differences between data and object URLs.

A data URL contains the data *within the URL*. The data (usually binary) is encoded in Base64 format and is appended to the URL itself.

An object URL represents some data that has been loaded into the browser's memory, usually Blobs and Files. It doesn't contain the data itself in the URL, but is a reference to the actual data. When you're done using it, an object URL can be revoked to prevent memory leaks.

10.4 Loading an Image with Drag and Drop

Problem

You want to be able to drag an image file into the browser window and display that image on the page when it is dropped.

Solution

Define an element to serve as the drop area, and a placeholder image element (see Example 10-8).

Example 10-8. The drop target and image elements

```
<label id="drop-target">
  <div>Drag and drop an image here</div>
  <input type="file" id="file-input">
</label>
<img id="placeholder">
```

Note that this example still includes a file input. This is so that those using assistive technologies can also upload an image without having to attempt a drag and drop operation. Because the drop target is a label, containing the file input, you can click anywhere inside the drop target to open the file chooser.

First, create a function that receives the image file and reads it as a data URL (see Example 10-9).

Example 10-9. Reading the dropped file

```
function showDroppedFile(file) {
  // Read the file data and insert the loaded image
  // into the page.
  const reader = new FileReader();
  reader.addEventListener('load', event => {
    const image = document.querySelector('#placeholder');
    image.src = event.target.result;
  });

  reader.readAsDataURL(file);
}
```

Next, create handler functions for the dragover and drop events. These events are attached to the drop target element (see Example 10-10).

Example 10-10. Adding the drag and drop code

```
const target = document.querySelector('#drop-target');
target.addEventListener('drop', event => {
  // Cancel the drop event. Otherwise, the browser will leave the page
  // and navigate to the file directly.
  event.preventDefault();

  // Get the selected file data. dataTransfer.items is a
  // DataTransferItemList. Each item in the list, a DataTransferItem, has data
  // about an item being dropped. As this example only deals with a single file, it
  // gets the first item in the list.
  const [item] = event.dataTransfer.items;

  // Get the dropped data as a File object.
  const file = item.getAsFile();

  // Only proceed if an image file was dropped.
  if (file.type.startsWith('image/')) {
    showDroppedFile(file);
  }
});

// You need to cancel the dragover event as well to prevent the
// file from replacing the full page content.
target.addEventListener('dragover', event => {
  event.preventDefault();
});
```

Finally, make sure to wire up the fallback file input. You just need to get the selected file, then pass it to the showDroppedFile method to provide the same result (see Example 10-11).

Example 10-11. Handling the file input

```
const fileInput = document.querySelector('#file-input');
fileInput.addEventListener('change', () => {
  const [file] = fileInput.files;
  showDroppedFile(file);
});
```

Discussion

By default, when you drag an image into a page, the browser navigates away from the current page. The URL changes to the path of the file, and the image is shown in the browser window. In this example, you instead want to load the image data into an <img> element and stay on the current page.

To prevent the default behavior, the drop handler calls `preventDefault` on the drop event. To fully prevent the behavior, you also need to call `preventDefault` on the `dragover` event, which is why you need the second event listener. This makes it so that the element can actually receive `drop` events.

10.5 Checking and Requesting Permissions

Problem

You want to check—and request if necessary—permissions to access a file on the local filesystem.

Solution

Show a file picker, and when a file is selected, call `queryPermission` to check for existing permission. If the permission check returns `prompt`, call `requestPermission` to show a permission request (see Example 10-12).

Example 10-12. Selecting and checking permissions for a file

```
/**
 * Selects a file, then checks permissions, showing a request if necessary,
 * for a file.
 * @return true if the file can be written to, false otherwise
 */
async function canAccessFile() {
  if ('showOpenFilePicker' in window) {
    // showOpenFilePicker can select multiple files, just
    // get the first one (with array destructuring).
    const [file] = window.showOpenFilePicker();

    let result = await file.queryPermission({ mode: 'readwrite' });
    if (result === 'prompt') {
      result = await file.requestPermission({ mode: 'readwrite' });
    }

    return result === 'granted';
  }

  // If you get here, it means the API isn't supported.
  return false;
}
```

This API may not be supported by all browsers yet. See CanIUse (*https://oreil.ly/AfNpL*) for the latest compatibility data.

Discussion

The `queryPermission` function returns either `granted` (the permission was previously granted), `denied` (access is denied), or `prompt` (need to ask for permission).

The requested mode is `readwrite`, which means the browser is able to write to your local filesystem if you grant the permission. This is why the permission check is important from a security and privacy perspective.

`queryPermission` checks the permission only and does not show a prompt. If this comes back as `prompt`, you can then call `requestPermission`, which shows a permission request in the browser. The file is considered writable if either call returns `granted`.

10.6 Exporting API Data to a File

Problem

You are requesting JSON data from an API, and you want to give the user an option to download the raw JSON data.

Solution

Let the user select an output file, then write the JSON data to the local filesystem.

This API may not be supported by all browsers yet. See CanIUse (*https://oreil.ly/tsT_j*) for the latest compatibility data.

First, define a helper function that shows the file picker and returns the file that was selected (see Example 10-13).

Example 10-13. Selecting an output file

```
/**
 * Shows a save file picker and returns the selected file handle.
 * @returns a file handle to the selected file, or null if the user clicked Cancel.
 */
```

```
async function selectOutputFile() {
  // Check to make sure the API is supported in this browser.
  if (!('showSaveFilePicker' in window)) {
    return null;
  }

  try {
    return window.showSaveFilePicker({
      // The default name for the output file
      suggestedName: 'users.json',

      // Limit the available file extensions.
      types: [
        { description: "JSON", accept: { "application/json": [".json"] } }
      ]
    });
  } catch (error) {
    // If the user clicks Cancel, an exception is thrown. In this case,
    // return null to indicate no file was selected.
    return null;
  }
}
```

Next, define a function that uses this helper, and perform the actual export (see Example 10-14).

Example 10-14. Exporting data to a local file

```
async function exportData(data) {
  // Use the helper function defined previously.
  const outputFile = await selectOutputFile();

  // Only proceed if an output file was actually selected.
  if (outputFile) {
    try {
      // Prepare a writable stream, which is used to save the file
      // to disk.
      const stream = await outputFile.createWritable();

      // Write the JSON t the stream in a human-readable format.
      await stream.write(JSON.stringify(userList, null, 2));
      await stream.close();

      // Show a success message.
      document.querySelector('#export-success').classList.remove('d-none');
    } catch (error) {
      console.error(error);
    }
  }
}
```

Discussion

This is a good approach for allowing a user to back up or export their data from your app. Some regulations, like the General Data Protection Regulation (GDPR) in the European Union, require you to make a user's data available for download.

In this case, text data is being written to the stream, which is of type `FileSystem WritableFileStream`. These streams also support writing `ArrayBuffer`, `TypedArray`, `DataView`, and `Blob` objects.

In order to create the text to write to the file, `exportData` is calling `JSON.stringify` with some extra arguments. The second `null` argument is the `replacer` function, which you saw in Chapter 2. This argument has to be provided in order to provide the third argument, which specifies the amount of indentation whitespace to apply. This creates a more readable output format.

At the time of writing, this API is still considered experimental. You should avoid using it in a production application until it has better browser support.

10.7 Exporting API Data with a Download Link

Problem

You want to provide export functionality but don't want to worry about filesystem permissions, like in Recipe 10.6.

Solution

Put the API data into a `Blob` object, and create an object URL to set as a link's `href` attribute. Then you can export the data with a normal browser file download, without needing filesystem permissions.

First, add a placeholder link to the page, which becomes the export link (see Example 10-15).

Example 10-15. The placeholder export link

```
<a id="export-link" download="users.json">Export User Data</a> ❶
```

❶ The `download` attribute provides a default filename to use when downloading.

After you fetch the data from the API and render it in the UI, create the `Blob` and object URL (see Example 10-16).

Example 10-16. Preparing the export link

```
const exportLink = document.querySelector('#export-link');

async function getUserData() {
  const response = await fetch('/api/users');
  const users = await response.json();

  // Render the user data in the UI, assuming that you
  // have a renderUsers function somewhere that does this.
  renderUsers(users);

  // Clean up the previous export data, if it exists.
  const currentUrl = exportLink.href;
  if (currentUrl) {
    URL.revokeObjectURL(currentUrl);
  }

  // Need a Blob for creating an object URL
  const blob = new Blob([JSON.stringify(userList, null, 2)], {
    type: 'application/json'
  });

  // The object URL links to the Blob contents—set this in the link.
  const url = URL.createObjectURL(blob);
  exportLink.href = url;
}
```

Discussion

This method of exporting requires no special permission. When the link is clicked, and it has the object URL set, it downloads the Blob's contents as a file, using the suggested filename of *users.json*.

A Blob is a special object that holds some piece data. Usually this is binary data like a file or image, but you can also create a Blob with string content, which is what this recipe does.

The Blob resides in memory, and the created object URL links to it. Once the object URL is set in the link element, it becomes an export download link. When the link is clicked, the object URL returns the raw string data. Since the link has a download attribute, it is downloaded to a local file.

To prevent memory leaks, clean up the old URL by calling URL.revokeObjectURL and passing the object URL as its argument. You can do this once you no longer need the object URL—for example, after the user downloads the file or before leaving the page.

10.8 Uploading a File with Drag and Drop

Problem

You want to allow the user to drag and drop a file, such as an image, then upload that file to a remote service.

Solution

Pass the received File object to the Fetch API in the handle for the drop event (see Example 10-17).

Example 10-17. Uploading a dropped file

```
const target = document.querySelector('.drop-target');

target.addEventListener('drop', event => {
  // Cancel the drop event. Otherwise, the browser will leave the page
  // and navigate to the file directly.
  event.preventDefault();

  // Get the selected file data.
  const [item] = event.dataTransfer.items;
  const file = item.getAsFile();

  if (file.type.startsWith('image/')) {
    fetch('/api/uploadFile', {
      method: 'POST',
      body: file
    });
  }
});

// You need to cancel the dragover event as well, to prevent the
// file from replacing the full page content.
target.addEventListener('dragover', event => {
  event.preventDefault();
});
```

Discussion

When you call getAsFile on the data transfer object, you get a File object. File extends from Blob, so you can use the Fetch API to send the file (Blob) contents to a remote server.

This example checks the MIME type of the uploaded file and will only upload it if it is an image file.

CHAPTER 11

Internationalization

11.0 Introduction

Modern browsers include a robust Internationalization API. This is a collection of APIs centered around language- or locale-specific tasks, such as:

- Formatting dates and times
- Formatting numbers
- Currency
- Pluralization rules

Before this API was available, you might have had to reach for a third-party library like Moment.js (for dates and times) or Numeral.js (for numbers). However, today's browsers support many of the same use cases, and you may not need these libraries in your app anymore.

Most of these APIs use the concept of a *locale*, which is usually a combination of a language and a region. For example, the locale for US English is en-US, and the locale for Canadian English is en-CA. You can use them with the default locale, which is the one being used by the browser, or you can specify a particular locale to format data appropriately for your desired region.

There is a new JavaScript date and time API in development called Temporal. At the time of writing, this is currently an ECMAScript proposal. It may become part of the language in the near future, but for the time being this book will cover the standard Date API.

11.1 Formatting a Date

Problem

You want to display a `Date` object in a format appropriate for the user's locale.

Solution

Use `Intl.DateTimeFormat` to format the `Date` object to a string value. Create the format object with two arguments: the desired locale and an options object where you can specify the format style. For dates, the supported format styles are (examples shown in the `en-US` locale):

- `short`: 10/16/23
- `medium`: Oct 16, 2023
- `long`: October 16, 2023
- `full`: Monday, October 16, 2023

To get the user's current locale, you can check the `navigator.language` property (see Example 11-1).

Example 11-1. Formatting a date

```
const formatter = new Intl.DateTimeFormat(navigator.language, { dateStyle: 'long' });
const formattedDate = formatter.format(new Date());
```

Discussion

You can also include the time information from a `Date` object by specifying a `timeStyle` property in the options object along with `dateStyle` (see Example 11-2).

Example 11-2. Formatting a date and time

```
const formatter = new Intl.DateTimeFormat(navigator.language, {
dateStyle: 'long', timeStyle: 'long' });
const formattedDateAndTime = formatter.format(new Date());
```

11.2 Getting the Parts of a Formatted Date

Problem

You want to split a formatted date into tokens. This is useful, for example, if you want to style different parts of the formatted date differently.

Solution

Use the `formatToParts` method of `Intl.DateTimeFormat` to format the date and return an array of tokens (see Example 11-3).

Example 11-3. Getting the parts of a formatted date

```
const formatter = new Intl.DateTimeFormat(navigator.language,
  { dateStyle: 'short' });
const parts = formatter.formatToParts(new Date());
```

Discussion

For a short date of `10/1/23`, the `parts` object shown in Example 11-3 looks like Example 11-4.

Example 11-4. The formatted date parts

```
[
  { type: 'month', value: '10' },
  { type: 'literal': value: '/' },
  { type: 'day': value: '1' },
  { type: 'literal', value: '/' },
  { type: 'year', value: '23' }
]
```

11.3 Formatting a Relative Date

Problem

You want to format the difference between a given date and today in an approximate, human-readable format. For example, you want a formatted string like "2 days ago" or "in 3 months."

Solution

Use `Intl.RelativeTimeFormat`. It has a `format` method that you call with a value offset, such as –2 (in the past) or 3 (in the future), and a unit such as "day," "month," etc. For example, calling `format(-2, *day*)` in the `en-US` locale results in the string "2 days ago."

This is actually a two-step process. `Intl.RelativeTimeFormat` doesn't directly calculate this between two dates. Rather, you need to first determine the offset and the unit to pass to the `format` method. The idea is to find the largest unit that differs between the two dates.

First, create a helper function that returns an object containing the offset and unit, as shown in Example 11-5.

Example 11-5. Finding the offset and unit

```
function getDateDifference(fromDate) {
  const today = new Date();

  if (fromDate.getFullYear() !== today.getFullYear()) {
    return { offset: fromDate.getFullYear() - today.getFullYear(), unit: 'year' };
  } else if (fromDate.getMonth() !== today.getMonth()) {
    return { offset: fromDate.getMonth() - today.getMonth(), unit: 'month' };
  } else {
    // You could even go more granular: down to hours, minutes, or seconds!
    return { offset: fromDate.getDate() - today.getDate(), unit: 'day' };
  }
}
```

This function returns an object with two properties: `offset` and `unit`, which you can pass to an `Intl.RelativeTimeFormat` (see Example 11-6).

Example 11-6. Formatting the relative date

```
function getRelativeDate(fromDate) {
  const { offset, unit } = getDateDifference(fromDate);
  const format = new Intl.RelativeTimeFormat();
  return format.format(offset, unit);
}
```

Here is the expected output if you called this function with the given dates on October 7, 2023 (keep in mind that when creating `Date` objects in this way, the months start at 0, but the days start at 1):

- October 1, 2023: `getRelativeDate(new Date(2023, 9, 1))`: "6 days ago"
- May 2, 2023: `getRelativeDate(new Date(2023, 4, 2))`: "5 months ago"
- June 2, 2025: `getRelativeDate(new Date(2025, 5, 2))`: "in 2 years"

Discussion

`getDateDifference` works by comparing the year, month, and day (in that order) of the given date with today's date, until it finds one that doesn't match. Then it returns the difference and the name of the unit, which are passed to the `Intl.RelativeTime Format`.

The `getRelativeDate` function doesn't give an exact relative time in months, days, hours, minutes, and seconds. It gives an approximation of the magnitude of the time difference.

Consider comparing May 2, 2023 to October 7, 2023. This is a difference of 5 months and 5 days, but `getRelativeDate` only says "5 months ago" as an approximation.

11.4 Formatting Numbers

Problem

You want to format a number with thousands separators and decimal places in a locale-specific way.

Solution

Pass the number to an `Intl.NumberFormat`'s `format` method. This method returns a string containing the formatted number.

By default, `Intl.NumberFormat` uses the default locale (assume that the default locale in Example 11-7 is `en-US`).

Example 11-7. Formatting a number in the default locale

```
// outputs '5,200.55' for en-US
console.log(
  new Intl.NumberFormat().format(5200.55)
);
```

You can also specify a different locale to the `Intl.NumberFormat` constructor (see Example 11-8).

Example 11-8. Formatting a number in the de-DE locale

```
// outputs '5.200,55'
console.log(
  new Intl.NumberFormat('de-DE').format(5200.55)
);
```

Discussion

`Intl.NumberFormat` applies locale-specific formatting rules to format individual numbers. You can also use it to format a range of numbers by passing two values to `formatRange`, as shown in Example 11-9.

Example 11-9. Formatting a range of numbers

```
// outputs '1,000-5,000' for en-US
console.log(
  new Intl.NumberFormat().formatRange(1000, 5000)
);
```

11.5 Rounding Decimal Places

Problem

You want to take a fractional number, which can have many decimal places, and round it to a set number of decimal places.

Solution

Use the `maximumFractionDigits` option to specify the number of digits after the decimal point. Example 11-10 shows how to round numbers to up to two decimal places.

Example 11-10. Rounding a number

```
function roundToTwoDecimalPlaces(number) {
  const format = new Intl.NumberFormat(navigator.language, {
    maximumFractionDigits: 2
  });

  return format.format(number);
}

// prints "5.49"
console.log(roundToTwoDecimalPlaces(5.49125));

// prints "5.5"
console.log(roundToTwoDecimalPlaces(5.49621));
```

11.6 Formatting a Price Range

Problem

Given an array of prices, stored as numbers, you want to create a formatted price range that reflects the low and high prices in the array.

Solution

Determine the minimum and maximum prices, then pass the style: *currency* option when creating an `Intl.NumberFormat`. Use this `Intl.NumberFormat` to create the range. You can also specify the currency to get the proper symbol in the output. Finally, call `formatRange` on the `Intl.NumberFormat` with the lower and upper price bounds (see Example 11-11).

Example 11-11. Formatting a price range

```
function formatPriceRange(prices) {
  const format = new Intl.NumberFormat(navigator.language, {
    style: 'currency'.

    // The currency code is required when using style: 'currency'.
    currency: 'USD'
  });
  return format.formatRange(
    // Find the lowest price in the array.
    Math.min(...prices),

    // Find the highest price in the array.
    Math.max(...prices)
  );
}

// outputs '$1.75–$11.00'
console.log(
  formatPriceRange([5.5, 3, 1.75, 11, 9.5])
);
```

Discussion

The `Math.max` and `Math.min` functions take multiple arguments, and they return the maximum or minimum from the whole set of those arguments. Example 11-11 uses the array spread syntax to pass all elements from the `prices` array to `Math.max` and `Math.min`.

11.7 Formatting Measurement Units

Problem

You want to format a number along with a measurement unit.

Solution

Use the `unit` style when creating the `Intl.NumberFormat` object, and specify the target unit. Example 11-12 shows how to format a number of gigabytes.

Example 11-12. Formatting gigabytes

```
const format = new Intl.NumberFormat(navigator.language, {
  style: 'unit',
  unit: 'gigabyte'
});

// prints "1,000 GB"
console.log(format.format(1000));
```

Discussion

You can also customize the unit label, by specifying the `unitDisplay` option to the `NumberFormat`. Possible values are:

`short`
Shows the abbreviated unit, separated with a space: `1,000 GB`

`narrow`
Shows the abbreviated unit, with no space: `1,000GB`

`long`
Shows the full unit name: `1,000 gigabytes`

11.8 Applying Pluralization Rules

Problem

You want to use the correct terminology when referring to different numbers of items. For example, consider a list of users. In English, you'd say "one user" (singular), but "three users" (plural). Other languages have more complex rules, and you want to make sure you cover these.

Solution

Use `Intl.PluralRules` to select the correct pluralized string.

First, construct an `Intl.PluralRules` object with the desired locale, and call its `select` method with the number of users (see Example 11-13).

Example 11-13. Determining the plural form

```
// An array containing the users
const users = getUsers();

const rules = new Intl.PluralRules('en-US');
const form = rules.select(users.length);
```

The select method returns a string depending on the plural form to be used and the specified locale. For the en-US locale, it returns either "one" (when the user count is one) or "other" (when the user count is not one). You can define messages using these values as a key, as shown in Example 11-14.

Example 11-14. A full plural rules solution

```
function formatUserCount(users) {
  // The variations of the message, depending
  // on the count
  const messages = {
    one: 'There is 1 user.',
    other: `There are ${users.length} users.`
  };

  // Use Intl.PluralRules to determine which message
  // should be displayed.
  const rules = new Intl.PluralRules('en-US');
  return messages[rules.select(users.length)];
}
```

Discussion

This solution requires knowing the different forms ahead of time so you can define the correct messages.

Intl.PluralRules also supports an ordinal mode, which works slightly differently. You can use this mode to format *ordinal* values like "1st," "2nd," "3rd," etc. The formatting rules vary from language to language, and you can map them to suffixes that you apply to the numbers.

For example, with the en-US locale, an ordinal Intl.PluralRules returns values such as:

- one for numbers ending in 1—"1st," "21st," etc.
- two for numbers ending in 2—"2nd, 42nd," etc.
- few for numbers ending in 3—"3rd, 33rd," etc.
- other for other numbers—"5th," "47th," etc.

11.9 Counting Characters, Words, and Sentences

Problem

You want to calculate the character, word, and sentence count of a string using locale-specific rules.

Solution

Use `Intl.Segmenter` to split the string and count the occurrences.

You can create a segmenter with grapheme (individual characters), word, or sentence granularity. The granularity determines the boundaries of the segments. Each segmenter can only have one granularity, so you need three segmenters (see Example 11-15).

Example 11-15. Getting the character, word, and sentence count of a string

```
function getCounts(text) {
  const characters = new Intl.Segmenter(
    navigator.language,
    { granularity: 'grapheme' }
  );

  const words = new Intl.Segmenter(
    navigator.language,
    { granularity: 'word' }
  );

  const sentences = new Intl.Segmenter(
    navigator.language,
    { granularity: 'sentence' }
  );

  // Convert each segment to an array, then get its length.
  return {
    characters: [...characters.segment(text)].length,
    words: [...words.segment(text)].length,
    sentences: [...sentences.segment(text)].length
  };
}
```

This API may not be supported by all browsers yet. See CanIUse (*https://oreil.ly/OL9G0*) for the latest compatibility data.

Discussion

When you call `segment` on a segmenter with some text, it returns an iterable object containing all of the segments. There are several ways to get the length of items in this iterable, but this example uses the array spread syntax, which creates an array containing all of the items. Then you just need to get the length of each array.

You may have solved this problem in the past by using the `split` method of a string. For example, you could split on whitespace to get an array of words and get the word count. This approach may work in your language, but the advantage of using `Intl.Segmenter` is that it takes the given locale's rules for breaking up words and sentences.

11.10 Formatting Lists

Problem

You have an array of items that you want to display in a comma-separated list. For example, an array of users is shown as "user1, user2, and user3."

Solution

Use `Intl.ListFormat` to combine the items into a list using the rules of the given locale. Example 11-16 uses an array of users, each of which has a `username` property.

Example 11-16. Formatting a list of user objects

```
function getUserListString(users, locale = 'en-US') {
  // The locale of the ListFormat is configurable.
  const listFormat = new Intl.ListFormat(locale);
  return listFormat.format(users.map(user => user.username));
}
```

Discussion

`Intl.ListFormat` adds words and punctuation as needed. For example, in the `en-US` locale, you get the following:

- 1 user: "user1"
- 2 users: "user1 and user2"
- 3 users: "user1, user2, and user3"

Here's another example using the `de-DE` locale:

- 1 user: "user1"
- 2 users: "user1 und user2"
- 3 users: "user1, user2 und user3"

Notice the use of "und" instead of "and," and also notice in the third case that there's no comma after user2 as there is in en-US. This is because German grammar does not use this comma (called the "Oxford comma").

As you can see, using `Intl.ListFormat` is much more robust than using an array's `join` method to join its values with a comma. That method, of course, does not take locale-specific rules into account.

11.11 Sorting an Array of Names

Problem

You have an array of names that you want to sort using locale-specific sorting rules.

Solution

Create an `Intl.Collator` to provide the comparison logic, then use its `compare` function to pass to `Array.prototype.sort` (see Example 11-17). This function compares two strings. It returns a negative value if the first string comes before the second, zero if the strings are equal, or a positive value if the first string comes after the second.

Example 11-17. Sorting an array of names with `Intl.Collator`

```
const names = [
  'Elena',
  'Mário',
  'André',
  'Renée',
  'Léo',
  'Olga',
  'Héctor',
]

const collator = new Intl.Collator();
names.sort(collator.compare);
```

A `Collator` can return any negative or positive value, not just necessarily –1 or 1.

Discussion

This is a concise way to sort an array of strings. Before `Intl.Collator`, you might have done something like Example 11-18.

Example 11-18. Sorting an array of strings directly

```
names.sort((a, b) => a.localeCompare(b));
```

This works fine, but one major difference is that you can't specify which locale's sorting rules to apply when comparing strings. Another benefit of `Intl.Collator` is its flexibility. You can fine-tune the logic it uses to compare strings.

For example, consider the array `[1, 2, 20, 3]`. Using the default collator, this would be the sorted order since it's using string comparison logic. You can pass the `numeric: true` option to `Intl.Collator`, and the sorted array then becomes `[1, 2, 3, 20]`.

CHAPTER 12

Web Components

12.0 Introduction

Web components are a way to build new HTML elements with their own behavior. This behavior is encapsulated in a *custom element*.

Creating a Component

You can create a web component by defining a class that extends HTMLElement, as shown in Example 12-1.

Example 12-1. A barebones web component

```
class MyComponent extends HTMLElement {
  connectedCallback() {
    this.textContent = 'Hello from MyComponent';
  }
}
```

When you add the custom element to the DOM, the browser calls the connectedCall back method. This is typically where most of your component's logic resides. This is one of the *lifecycle callbacks*. Some other lifecycle callbacks include:

disconnectedCallback
    Called when you remove the custom element from the DOM. This is a good place to do cleanup, such as removing event listeners.

attributeChangedCallback
    Called when you change one of the element's watched attributes.

Registering a Custom Element

Once you've created your custom element class, you must register it with the browser before using it in an HTML document. You can register your custom element by calling `define` on the global `customElements` object, as shown in Example 12-2.

Example 12-2. Registering a custom element with the browser

```
customElements.define('my-component', MyComponent);
```

If you try to define a custom element that has already been defined, the browser throws an error. If this is a possibility for you, you can call `customElements.get('my-component')` in order to check if it's already defined. If this returns `undefined`, it's safe to call `customElements.define`.

Once you register the element, you can use it like any other HTML element, as shown in Example 12-3.

Example 12-3. Using the custom element

```
<my-component></my-component>
```

Custom elements must always have a hyphenated name. This is required by the specification. They also must always have a closing tag, even if there is no child content.

Templates

There are several ways to get HTML markup into a web component. For example, in the `connectedCallback`, you can manually create elements by calling `document.crea teElement` and manually appending them.

You can also specify a component's markup with a `<template>` element. This contains some HTML that you'll use during the `connectedCallback` to give your component its content. These templates are very simple—they don't support data binding, variable interpolation, or any kind of logic. They only serve as a starting point of the HTML content. Within the `connectedCallback`, you can select elements, set dynamic values, and add event listeners as needed.

Slots

A `<slot>` is a special element you can use in a template. A slot is a placeholder for some child content that is passed in. A component can have a default slot as well as one or more *named* slots. You can use named slots to place multiple pieces of content inside your component.

Example 12-4 shows a simple template that has a named and default slot.

Example 12-4. A template with slots

```
<template>
  <h2><slot name="name"></slot></h2>
  <slot></slot>
</template>
```

Suppose this template is used in an `<author-bio>` component, as shown in Example 12-5.

Example 12-5. Specifying content for slots

```
<author-bio>
  <span slot="name">John Doe</span>
  <p>John is a great author who has written many books.</p>
</author-bio>
```

In the component's child content, you can specify a `slot` attribute that corresponds to a named slot in the component template. The `span` element containing the text "John Doe" will be placed in the component's `name` slot, inside the `h2` element. Any other child content, without a `slot` element, is placed in the default slot (the one with no name).

Shadow DOM

A shadow DOM is a collection of elements that are isolated from the rest of the main DOM. Web components use shadow DOM extensively. One main advantage of using shadow DOM is for scoped CSS styles. Any styles you define in a shadow DOM *only* apply to elements inside that shadow DOM. Other elements in the document, even if they'd normally match the selector of a CSS rule, do not have the CSS applied.

This style scoping goes both ways. If you have global styles on your page, they will not apply to any of the elements in a shadow DOM.

A shadow DOM, created by attaching a *shadow root* to a web component, can be open or closed. When a shadow DOM is open, you can access and modify its elements with JavaScript. When it is closed, a web component's shadowRoot property is null so you can't access the content within.

Light DOM

Using shadow DOM is completely optional, however. The *Light DOM* refers to the regular, non-encapsulated DOM inside the web component. Because Light DOM is not encapsulated from the rest of the page, global styles will be applied to its child elements.

12.1 Creating a Component to Show Today's Date

Problem

You want a web component that formats and shows today's date in the browser's locale.

Solution

Use Intl.DateTimeFormat inside the web component to format the current date (see Example 12-6).

Example 12-6. A custom element that formats the current date

```
class TodaysDate extends HTMLElement {
  connectedCallback() {
    const formatter = new Intl.DateTimeFormat(
      navigator.language,
      { dateStyle: 'full' }
    );

    this.textContent = formatter.format(new Date());
  }
}

customElements.define('todays-date', TodaysDate);
```

Now you can show today's date by using this web component without any attributes or child content, as shown in Example 12-7.

Example 12-7. Showing the current date

```
<p>
  Today's date is: <todays-date></todays-date>
</p>
```

Discussion

When a `<todays-date>` element enters the DOM, the browser calls the `connected Callback` method. In the `connectedCallback`, the `TodaysDate` class formats the current date with an `Intl.DateTimeFormat` object, which you may remember from Chapter 11. The `connectedCallback` sets this formatted date string as the element's `textContent`, which is inherited from `Node` (an ancestor of `HTMLElement`).

12.2 Creating a Component to Format a Custom Date

Problem

You want a web component that formats an arbitrary date value.

Solution

Give the web component a `date` attribute, and use this to generate the formatted date (see Example 12-8). You can watch this attribute for changes and reformat the date if the date attribute changes.

Example 12-8. A custom date component

```
class DateFormatter extends HTMLElement {
  // The browser will only notify the component about changes, via the
  // attributeChangedCallback, for attributes that are listed here.
  static observedAttributes = ['date'];

  constructor() {
    super();

    // Create the format here so you don't have to
    // re-create it every time the date changes.
    this.formatter = new Intl.DateTimeFormat(
      navigator.language,
      { dateStyle: 'full' }
    );
  }

  /**
   * Formats the date represented by the current value of the 'date'
   * attribute, if any.
   */
  formatDate() {
    if (this.hasAttribute('date')) {
      this.textContent = this.formatter.format(
        new Date(this.getAttribute('date'))
      );
    } else {
```

```
    // If no date specified, show nothing.
    this.textContent = '';
    }
  }

  attributeChangedCallback() {
    // Only watching one attribute, so this must be a change
    // to the date attribute. Update the formatted date, if any.
    this.formatDate();
  }

  connectedCallback() {
    // The element was just added. Show the initial formatted date, if any.
    this.formatDate();
  }
}

customElements.define('date-formatter', DateFormatter);
```

You can now pass a date to the `date` attribute to get it formatted in the user's locale (see Example 12-9).

Example 12-9. Using the `date-formatter` element

```
<date-formatter date="2023-10-16T03:52:49.955Z"></date-formatter>
```

Discussion

This recipe expands on Recipe 12.1 by adding the ability to specify your own date via an attribute.

By default, if you change the value of an attribute passed to a custom element, nothing happens. The logic in `connectedCallback` only runs when you first add the component to the DOM. To make the component react to attribute changes, you can implement the `attributeChangedCallback` method. In the `date-formatter` component, this method takes the updated `date` attribute and create a new formatted date. When an attribute changes, the browser calls this method with the attribute name, the old value, and the new value.

However, this alone won't solve the problem. If you just implement `attribute ChangedCallback`, you still won't be notified of attribute changes. This is because the browser only calls `attributeChangedCallback` for *observed* attributes. This lets you define a subset of attributes so the browser only calls `attributeChangedCallback` for those attributes you're interested in. To define these attributes, add a static `observedAttributes` property to your component class. This should be an array of attribute names.

In the `date-formatter` component, you're only watching one attribute (the `date` attribute). Because of this, in `attributeChangedCallback` you don't need to check the `name` argument since you already know it's the `date` attribute that changed. In a component with multiple watched attributes, you can check the `name` to find out which attribute has changed.

If you change the value of the `date` attribute with JavaScript, the `attributeChanged Callback` will run and update the formatted date.

12.3 Creating a Feedback Component

Problem

You want to create a reusable component where a user can provide feedback about whether or not the page is helpful.

Solution

Create a web component to present the feedback buttons and dispatch a custom event when the user clicks on one.

First, you need to create a template element to contain the markup that this component uses, as shown in Example 12-10.

Example 12-10. Creating the template

```
const template = document.createElement('template');
template.innerHTML = `
  <style>
    .feedback-prompt {
      display: flex;
      align-items: center;
      gap: 0.5em;
    }

    button {
      padding: 0.5em 1em;
    }
  </style>

  <div class="feedback-prompt">
    <p>Was this helpful?</p>
    <button type="button" data-helpful="true">Yes</button>
    <button type="button" data-helpful="false">No</button>
  </div>
`;
```

This component uses a shadow DOM that contains the template markup (see Example 12-11). The CSS style rules are scoped to this component only.

Example 12-11. The component implementation

```
class FeedbackRating extends HTMLElement {
  constructor() {
    super();

    // Create the shadow DOM and render the template into it.
    const shadowRoot = this.attachShadow({ mode: 'open' });
    shadowRoot.appendChild(template.content.cloneNode(true));
  }

  connectedCallback() {
    this.shadowRoot.querySelector('.feedback-prompt').addEventListener('click',
    event => {
      const { helpful } = event.target.dataset;

      if (typeof helpful !== 'undefined') {
        // Once a feedback option is chosen, hide the buttons and show a
        // confirmation.
        this.shadowRoot.querySelector('.feedback-prompt').remove();
        this.shadowRoot.textContent = 'Thanks for your feedback!';

        // JavaScript doesn't have a 'parseBoolean' type function, so convert the
        // string value to the corresponding boolean value.
        this.helpful = helpful === 'true';

        // Dispatch a custom event, so your app can be notified when a feedback
        // button is clicked.
        this.shadowRoot.dispatchEvent(new CustomEvent('feedback', {
          composed: true, // This is needed to "escape" the shadow DOM boundary.
          bubbles: true // This is needed to propagate up the DOM.
        }));
      }
    });
  }
}

customElements.define('feedback-rating', FeedbackRating);
```

Now you can add this feedback component to your app (see Example 12-12).

Example 12-12. Using the feedback-rating component

```
<h2>Feedback</h2>
<feedback-rating></feedback-rating>
```

You can listen for the custom `feedback` event to be notified when the user selects a feedback option (see Example 12-13). It's up to you what to do with this information; maybe you want to send the data to an analytics endpoint with the Fetch API.

Example 12-13. Listening for the feedback event

```
document.querySelector('feedback-rating').addEventListener('feedback', event => {
  // Get the value of the feedback component's "helpful" property and send it to an
  // endpoint with a POST request.
  fetch('/api/analytics/feedback', {
    method: 'POST',
    body: JSON.stringify({ helpful: event.target.helpful }),
    headers: {
      'Content-Type': 'application/json'
    }
  });
});
```

Discussion

The `feedback-rating` component presents a prompt and two buttons. The user clicks one of the two buttons depending on whether they think the website content is helpful or not.

The `click` event listener uses event delegation. Instead of adding a listener to each button, it adds a single listen that responds to a click anywhere inside the feedback prompt. If the clicked element does not have a `data-helpful` attribute, then the user must not have clicked on a feedback button, so do nothing. Otherwise, it converts the string value to a boolean and sets it as a property on the custom element that can be retrieved later. It also dispatches an event that you can listen for elsewhere.

In order for this event to cross the shadow DOM into the regular DOM, you must set the `composed: true` option. Otherwise, any event listener that you added to the custom element won't be triggered.

Once that event is triggered, you can check the feedback element itself (available as the `event.target` property) for the `helpful` property to determine which feedback button the user clicked.

Because the styles and markup are contained in a shadow DOM, the CSS rules do not affect any elements outside of the shadow DOM. This is important to note, as otherwise an element selector like `button` would style every button on the page. Because the styles are scoped, they are only applied to buttons inside the custom element.

However, the content passed to the component's slots *can* be styled by global CSS rules. The slotted content does not move into the shadow DOM, but rather remains in the standard, or light, DOM.

12.4 Creating a Profile Card Component

Problem

You want to create a reusable card component to show a user profile.

Solution

Use slots in your web component to pass content to certain regions.

First, define the template with some styles and markup, as shown in Example 12-14.

Example 12-14. The profile card template

```
const template = document.createElement('template');
template.innerHTML = `
  <style>
    :host {
      display: grid;
      border: 1px solid #ccc;
      border-radius: 5px;
      padding: 8px;
      grid-template-columns: auto 1fr;
      column-gap: 16px;
      align-items: center;
      margin: 1rem;
    }

    .photo {
      border-radius: 50%;
      grid-row: 1 / span 3;
    }

    .name {
      font-size: 2rem;
      font-weight: bold;
    }

    .title {
      font-weight: bold;
    }
  </style>

  <div class="photo"><slot name="photo"></slot></div>
  <div class="name"><slot name="name"></slot></div>
  <div class="title"><slot name="title"></slot></div>
  <div class="bio"><slot></slot></div>
`;
```

This template has three named slots (photo, name, and title) and one default slot for the biography. The component implementation itself is rather minimal; it just creates and attaches a shadow root with the template (see Example 12-15).

Example 12-15. The component implementation

```
class ProfileCard extends HTMLElement {
  constructor() {
    super();
    this.attachShadow({ mode: 'open' });
    this.shadowRoot.appendChild(template.content.cloneNode(true));
  }
}

customElements.define('profile-card', ProfileCard);
```

To use the component, you can specify the slot attribute on child elements to specify which slot the content should go into (see Example 12-16). The biography element, which does not have a slot attribute, is placed in the default slot.

Example 12-16. Using the profile card

```
<profile-card>
  <img slot="photo" src="/api/portraits/chavez.jpg" />
  <div slot="name">Phillip Chavez</div>
  <div slot="title">CEO</div>
  <p>Philip is a great CEO.</p>
</profile-card>

<profile-card>
  <img slot="photo" src="/api/portraits/lynch.jpg" />
  <div slot="name">Jamie Lynch</div>
  <div slot="title">Vice President</div>
  <p>Jamie is a great vice president.</p>
</profile-card>
```

Figure 12-1 shows the rendered result of the profile card component.

Phillip Chavez

CEO

Phillip is a great CEO.

Figure 12-1. The rendered profile card

Discussion

In the CSS styles, you might have noticed the :host selector, which represents styles that are applied to the custom element's *shadow host*. This is the element that the shadow DOM is attached to.

With this example, you can see how web components let you create reusable content and layouts. Slots are a powerful tool that enables you to insert content exactly where it's needed.

12.5 Creating a Lazy Loading Image Component

Problem

You want a reusable component that contains an image that isn't loaded until it scrolls into the viewport.

Solution

Use an IntersectionObserver to wait for the element to scroll into view, then set the src element on the contained image.

This recipe adapts Recipe 6.1 from Chapter 6, presenting its solution inside a web component (see Examples 12-17 and 12-18).

Example 12-17. The LazyImage component

```
class LazyImage extends HTMLElement {
  constructor() {
    super();

    const shadowRoot = this.attachShadow({ mode: 'open' });
    this.image = document.createElement('img');
    shadowRoot.appendChild(this.image);
  }

  connectedCallback() {
    const observer = new IntersectionObserver(entries => {
      if (entries[0].isIntersecting) {
        console.log('Loading image');
        this.image.src = this.getAttribute('src');
        observer.disconnect();
      }
    });

    observer.observe(this);
  }
}
```

```
customElements.define('lazy-image', LazyImage);
```

Example 12-18. Using the LazyImage component

```
<lazy-image src="https://placekitten.com/200/138"></lazy-image>
```

Discussion

Once the element scrolls into view, the `IntersectionObserver` callback gets the `src` attribute and sets it as the image's `src` attribute, which triggers the image to load.

> This example illustrates how to create a custom element that extends a built-in element, but for lazy loading images you may not need it. Newer browsers support the `loading="lazy"` attribute on `img` tags, which has the same effect—the image is not loaded until it scrolls into view.

12.6 Creating a Disclosure Component

Problem

You want to show or hide some content by clicking a button. For example, you may have an "Advanced" section of a form that is collapsed by default, but can be expanded by clicking a button.

Solution

Build a disclosure web component. The component has two parts: the button that toggles the content, and the content itself. Each of these two parts will have a slot. The default slot will be for the content, and there will be a named slot for the button. This component can also be expanded or collapsed programmatically by changing the value of its `open` attribute.

First, define the template for the disclosure component, as shown in Example 12-19.

Example 12-19. The disclosure component template

```
const template = document.createElement('template');
template.innerHTML = `
  <div>
    <button type="button" class="toggle-button">
      <slot name="title"></slot>
    </button>
    <div class="content">
```

```
      <slot></slot>
    </div>
  </div>
`;
```

The component implementation is shown in Example 12-20.

Example 12-20. The disclosure component implementation

```
class Disclosure extends HTMLElement {
  // Watch the 'open' attribute to react to changes.
  static observedAttributes = ['open'];

  constructor() {
    super();
    this.attachShadow({ mode: 'open' });
    this.shadowRoot.appendChild(template.content.cloneNode(true));

    this.content = this.shadowRoot.querySelector('.content');
  }

  connectedCallback() {
    this.content.hidden = !this.hasAttribute('open');
    this.shadowRoot.querySelector('.toggle-button')
      .addEventListener('click', () => {
        if (this.hasAttribute('open')) {
          // Content is currently showing; remove the 'open'
          // attribute and hide the content.
          this.removeAttribute('open');
          this.content.hidden = true;
        } else {
          // Content is currently hidden; add the 'open' attribute
          // and show the content.
          this.setAttribute('open', '');
          this.content.hidden = false;
        }
      });
  }

  attributeChangedCallback(name, oldValue, newValue) {
    // Update the content's hidden state based on the new attribute value.
    if (newValue !== null) {
      this.content.hidden = false;
    } else {
      this.content.hidden = true;
    }
  }
}

// The element name must be hyphenated.
customElements.define('x-disclosure', Disclosure);
```

One last thing—you need to add a small bit of CSS to the page. Otherwise, the child content will flicker on the page for a moment, then disappear. This is because before the custom element is registered, it has no behavior, and the browser isn't aware of its slots. This means that any child content will be rendered in the page.

Then, once the custom element is defined, the child content moves into the slot and disappears.

To fix this, you can use CSS to hide the element's content until it is registered by using the :defined pseudo-class.

Example 12-21. Fixing the flicker issue

```
x-disclosure:not(:defined) {
  display: none;
}
```

This will initially hide the content. Once the custom element becomes defined, the element is shown. You won't see the flicker because the content has already been moved to the slot.

Finally, you can use the disclosure element, as shown in Example 12-22.

Example 12-22. Using the disclosure element

```
<x-disclosure>
  <div slot="title">Details</div>
  This is the detail child content that will be expanded or collapsed
  when clicking the title button.
</x-disclosure>
```

The toggle button will have the text "Details," since that is placed in the title slot. The remaining content is placed in the default slot.

Discussion

The disclosure component uses its open attribute to determine whether or not to show the child content. When the toggle button is clicked, it adds or removes the attribute depending on the current state, then conditionally applies the hidden attribute to the child content.

You can also programmatically toggle the child content by adding or removing the open attribute. This works because the component is observing the open attribute. If you change it with JavaScript, or even in the browser developer tools, the browser calls the component's attributeChangedCallback method with the new value.

The open attribute does not have a value. If you want the content to be open by default, simply add the open attribute with no value, as shown in Example 12-23.

Example 12-23. Showing the content by default

```
<x-disclosure open>
  <div slot="title">Details</div>
  This is the detail child content that will be expanded or collapsed
  when clicking the title button.
</x-disclosure>
```

If you remove the attribute, the newValue argument to attributeChangedCallback will be null. In that case, it will hide the child content by applying the hidden attribute. If you add the attribute with no value, as shown in Example 12-23, the new Value argument will be an empty string. If that's the case, it will remove the hidden attribute.

12.7 Creating a Styled Button Component

Problem

You want to create a reusable button component with different style options.

Solution

There will be three variants of the button:

- the default variant, with a gray background
- the "primary" variant, with a blue background
- the "danger" variant, with a red background

First, create the template with the custom button styling, along with CSS classes for the "primary" and "danger" variants, as shown in Example 12-24.

Example 12-24. The button template

```
const template = document.createElement('template');
template.innerHTML = `
  <style>
    button {
      background: #333;
      padding: 0.5em 1.25em;
      font-size: 1rem;
      border: none;
      border-radius: 5px;
```

```
      color: white;
    }

    button.primary {
      background: #2563eb;
    }

    button.danger {
      background: #dc2626;
    }
  </style>

  <button>
    <slot></slot>
  </button>
`;
```

Most of this template is the CSS. The actual markup for the component itself is quite simple: just a button element with a default slot.

The component itself will support two attributes:

variant

The name of the button variant (primary or danger)

type

The type attribute that is passed into the underlying button element. Set this to button to prevent submitting a form (see Example 12-25).

Example 12-25. The button component

```
class StyledButton extends HTMLElement {
  static observedAttributes = ['variant', 'type'];

  constructor() {
    super();
    this.attachShadow({ mode: 'open' });
    this.shadowRoot.appendChild(template.content.cloneNode(true));
    this.button = this.shadowRoot.querySelector('button');
  }

  attributeChangedCallback(name, oldValue, newValue) {
    if (name === 'variant') {
      this.button.className = newValue;
    } else if (name === 'type') {
      this.button.type = newValue;
    }
  }
}

customElements.define('styled-button', StyledButton);
```

To add a click listener, you actually don't have to do any further work. You can add a click listener to the `styled-button` element and it will be triggered when you click the underlying button, thanks to event delegation. With event delegation, you can add an event listener to a parent element, and events on its children will also trigger the parent's event listener.

Finally, here is how you use the `styled-button` component (see Example 12-26).

Example 12-26. Using the `styled-button` component

```
<styled-button id="default-button" type="button">Default</styled-button>
<styled-button id="primary-button" type="button" variant="primary">
  Primary
</styled-button>
<styled-button id="danger-button" type="button" variant="danger">
  Danger
</styled-button>
```

Discussion

The styling is applied by setting a class name on the button element equal to the variant name. This will cause the corresponding CSS rule to apply the desired background color.

You don't need to have any code in the `connectedCallback` to apply the class, because the browser will call the `attributeChangedCallback` with the initial values as well as any subsequently updated values.

You can add a click event listener to the `styled-button` in the same way as you would a normal button (see Example 12-27).

Example 12-27. Adding a click listener

```
<script>
document.querySelector('#default-button').addEventListener('click', () => {
  console.log('Clicked the default button');
});
</script>

<styled-button id="default-button" type="button">Default</styled-button>
```

CHAPTER 13

UI Elements

13.0 Introduction

Modern browsers have a few powerful built-in UI elements that you can use in your app. These UI components previously required third-party libraries (or you could build your own).

Dialogs

Pop-up dialogs are a mainstay of many apps, providing feedback and prompting for input. There are countless dialog libraries out there, and it's possible to build your own. Modern browsers have already done this for you with the `<dialog>` element. This is a pop-up dialog and includes a backdrop that covers the rest of the page. You can apply styles to both the backdrop and the dialog with a little CSS. By default, the dialog is just a box that pops up with the backdrop behind it. It's up to you to add a title, buttons, and other content.

Some dialogs contain multiple buttons, and you want to run different code depending on which option they chose. For example, a confirmation modal might have Confirm and Cancel buttons. You'll need to handle this yourself as well, adding click event listeners to the buttons. In each event listener, you can close the dialog by calling `close` on it. The `close` method is a built-in method on the dialog that takes an optional argument that lets you specify a "return value." This can be checked later from the dialog's `returnValue` property. This lets you pass data from the dialog back to the page that opened it.

Details

A <details> element is a component whose content is collapsible. It has some summary content that is displayed in an interactive element. By clicking this element, you can show or hide the detailed content. Like with dialogs, you can style the component with CSS and toggle its visibility with JavaScript.

Popovers

A popover is similar to a dialog. This is another type of pop-up element. There are a few differences between a popover and a dialog:

- Clicking outside of the popover will close it.
- You can still interact with the rest of the page while a popover is visible.
- You can turn any HTML element into a popover.

Notifications

Smartphones use notifications extensively, and newer operating systems also support notifications. Modern browsers have an API for showing native operating system notifications, triggered from JavaScript. The user must grant permission before these notifications can be sent. These notifications are created in your JavaScript code, on demand, while the app is running.

13.1 Creating an Alert Dialog

Problem

You want to show a dialog with a simple message, with an OK button to close it.

Solution

Use a <dialog> element with an OK button.

This API may not be supported by older browsers. See CanIUse (*https://oreil.ly/tk52g*) for the latest compatibility data.

First, define the HTML for your dialog, as shown in Example 13-1.

Example 13-1. The dialog markup

```
<dialog id="alert">
  <h2>Alert</h2>
  <p>This is an alert dialog.</p>

  <button type="button" id="ok-button">OK</button>
</dialog>

<button type="button" id="show-dialog">Show Dialog</button>
```

You need two snippets of JavaScript. First, you'll need a function to trigger the dialog to be displayed, and then you'll need an event listener for the OK button to close the dialog (see Example 13-2).

Example 13-2. JavaScript for the dialog

```
// Select the dialog, its OK button, and the trigger button elements.
const dialog = document.querySelector('#alert');
const okButton = document.querySelector('#ok-button');
const trigger = document.querySelector('#show-dialog');

// Close the dialog when the OK button is clicked.
okButton.addEventListener('click', () => {
  dialog.close();
});

// Show the dialog when the trigger button is clicked.
trigger.addEventListener('click', () => {
  dialog.showModal();
});
```

This results in the dialog shown in Figure 13-1.

Figure 13-1. The alert dialog

Discussion

The dialog's `showModal` method shows a *modal* dialog. A modal dialog blocks the rest of the page until it is closed. This means if you open a modal dialog, clicking on other elements on the page will have no effect. With a modal dialog, the focus is "trapped" inside the dialog. Using the Tab key will cycle focus through the focusable elements in the dialog only. If this isn't what you want, you can also call the `show` method. This will show a *modeless* dialog, which still allows you to interact with the rest of the page while the dialog is open.

Clicking the OK button will close the dialog due to the click listener calling `dialog.close`, but you can also close the modal by pressing the Escape key. To capture this, you can listen for the dialog's `cancel` event. Canceling the dialog with the Escape key will also trigger the dialog's `close` event. Finally, closing the dialog manually by calling `close` on it will trigger the `close` event as well.

The `dialog` element also has some nice keyboard accessibility features. When you click the Show Dialog button and the dialog opens, the first focusable element button automatically receives focus. In this case, it's the OK button. You can change this behavior by adding the `autofocus` attribute to the element that you want to receive the initial focus when the dialog is opened.

When you close the dialog, either by pressing the Escape key or clicking the OK button, the keyboard focus will return to the Show Dialog button.

You can style both the dialog itself and its semitransparent backdrop with CSS. For the dialog, you can add a CSS rule targeting the `<dialog>` element itself. To style the backdrop—for example, you might want it to be a more opaque black—you can use the `::backdrop` pseudo-element (see Example 13-3).

Example 13-3. Styling the backdrop

```
#alert::backdrop {
  background: rgba(0, 0, 0, 0.75);
}
```

13.2 Creating a Confirmation Dialog

Problem

You want to prompt the user to confirm an operation. The prompt should show a question and have Confirm and Cancel buttons.

Solution

This is another great use case for a `<dialog>`. First, create your dialog content with the prompt and buttons, as shown in Example 13-4.

Example 13-4. The confirmation dialog markup

```
<dialog id="confirm">
  <h2>Confirm</h2>
  <p>Are you sure you want to do that?</p>

  <button type="button" class="confirm-button">Confirm</button>
  <button type="button" class="cancel-button">Cancel</button>
</dialog>
```

 This API may not be supported by all browsers yet. See CanIUse (*https://oreil.ly/tk52g*) for the latest compatibility data.

You want both buttons to close the dialog, but to take different actions. To do this, you can pass a string argument to `dialog.close`. This will set the `returnValue` property on the dialog itself, which you can examine when you receive the `close` event (see Example 13-3).

Example 13-5. Event listeners for the confirmation dialog

```
const dialog = document.querySelector('#confirm');

confirmButton.addEventListener('click', () => {
  // Close the dialog with a return value of 'confirm'
  dialog.close('confirm');
});

cancelButton.addEventListener('click', () => {
  // Close the dialog with a return value of 'cancel'
  dialog.close('cancel');
});

dialog.addEventListener('cancel', () => {
  // Canceling with the Escape key doesn't set a return value.
  // Set it to 'cancel' here so the close event handler will get
  // the proper value.
  dialog.returnValue = 'cancel';
});

dialog.addEventListener('close', () => {
```

```
  if (dialog.returnValue === 'confirm') {
    // The user clicked the Confirm button.
    // Perform the action, such as creating or deleting data.
  } else {
    // The user clicked the Cancel button or pressed the Escape key.
    // Don't perform the action.
  }
});
```

The resulting confirmation dialog looks like Figure 13-2.

Figure 13-2. The confirmation dialog

Discussion

If the user clicks one of the buttons, the dialog is closed with a return value that depends on which button was clicked. After the dialog closes, it will emit the close event where you can check the returnValue property. If the returnValue is confirm, you know the user clicked the Confirm button. Otherwise, the returnValue is cancel and you can cancel the operation.

This example also listens for the cancel event. This event is triggered if the dialog is closed by pressing the Escape key. When the dialog is closed in this way, the dialog's returnValue is not updated and will retain whatever previous value it had. To make sure the returnValue is correct, the cancel event handler sets it. This works because the close event is triggered *after* the cancel event. Because the Escape key triggers this event, you don't need to actually listen for the Escape key to be pressed.

Why do you need to handle this case? Well, if you close the dialog, it is not destroyed. It still exists in the DOM, just hidden, and still has the same returnValue set. Suppose you opened the dialog previously, and you clicked Confirm. The return value is now set to confirm. If you open the confirmation dialog again and cancel by pressing Escape, the return value will still be confirm when the close event is handled. To avoid this potential bug, you can use the cancel event handler to explicitly set the returnValue to cancel.

13.3 Creating a Confirmation Dialog Web Component

Problem

You want to create a customizable confirmation dialog. When you show the dialog, you want to get a `Promise` that resolves to the return value rather than having to listen for multiple events.

Solution

Wrap the dialog in a web component, using a slot for the confirmation message. The component exposes a `showConfirmation` method that uses a `Promise`.

> This API may not be supported by all browsers yet. See CanIUse (*https://oreil.ly/tk52g*) for the latest compatibility data.

As with most web components, start by defining the template, as shown in Example 13-6.

Example 13-6. The template for the confirmation dialog component

```
const template = document.createElement('template');
template.innerHTML = `
  <dialog id="confirm">
    <h2>Confirm</h2>
    <p><slot></slot></p>

    <button type="button" class="confirm-button">Confirm</button>
    <button type="button" class="cancel-button">Cancel</button>
  </dialog>
`;
```

The template contains a slot that will receive the component's child content. Next, Example 13-7 show the component implementation.

Example 13-7. The confirmation component implementation

```
class ConfirmDialog extends HTMLElement {
  connectedCallback() {
    const shadowRoot = this.attachShadow({ mode: 'open' });
    shadowRoot.appendChild(template.content.cloneNode(true));

    this.dialog = shadowRoot.querySelector('dialog');
    this.dialog.addEventListener('cancel', () => {
```

```
      this.dialog.returnValue = 'cancel';
    });

    shadowRoot.querySelector('.confirm-button')
      .addEventListener('click', () => {
        this.dialog.close('confirm');
      });

    shadowRoot.querySelector('.cancel-button')
      .addEventListener('click', () => {
        this.dialog.close('cancel');
      });
  }

  showConfirmation() {
    this.dialog.showModal();

    return new Promise(resolve => {
      // Listen for the next close event and resolve the Promise.
      // Resolve the Promise with a boolean indicating whether or not the
      // user confirmed.
      this.dialog.addEventListener('close', () => {
        resolve(this.dialog.returnValue === 'confirm');
      }, {
        // Only listen for the event once, then remove the listener.
        once: true
      });
    });
  }
}

customElements.define('confirm-dialog', ConfirmDialog);
```

Suppose you want to use this component to confirm a delete operation. You can add the element to your page with the confirmation prompt as the child content (see Example 13-8).

Example 13-8. The component markup

```
<confirm-dialog id="confirm-delete">
  Are you sure you want to delete this item?
</confirm-dialog>
```

To show the dialog, select the DOM element and call its showConfirmation method. Await the returned Promise to get the return value (see Example 13-9).

Example 13-9. Using the confirmation dialog component

```
const confirmDialog = document.querySelector('#confirm-delete');
if (await confirmDialog.showConfirmation()) {
```

```
  // perform the delete operation
}
```

As with Recipe 12.6 from Chapter 12, you need to add some CSS to hide the child content until it is placed within the slots to prevent a flicker of the dialog content (see Example 13-10).

Example 13-10. Fixing the flicker issue

```
confirm-dialog:not(:defined) {
  display: none;
}
```

Discussion

This is a good example of the usefulness of web components to encapsulate custom behavior. In this case, you also added a custom method to be called from the outside. This method shows the dialog and abstracts away having to listen for multiple events. You just show the dialog and wait for the result.

13.4 Using a Disclosure Element

Problem

You have some content you want to show or hide using a toggle button.

Solution

Use the built-in <details> element (see Example 13-10).

Example 13-11. Using the details element

```
<details>
  <summary>More Info</summary>
  Here are some extra details that you can toggle.
</details>
```

When the details are collapsed, you'll just see the More Info trigger button, as shown in Figure 13-3.

> ▶ More Info

Figure 13-3. The collapsed details element

When you click the summary, the details open and the arrow changes to indicate that the content is expanded, as shown in Figure 13-4.

> ▼ More Info
>
> Lorem ipsum dolor sit amet, consectetur adipiscing elit.
> Donec eget ex id dolor tempor tincidunt. Duis fermentum
> enim sapien, eu auctor massa efficitur quis. Vestibulum
> auctor turpis id ultrices finibus. Morbi ex mi, porttitor sit
> amet lacus vel, viverra tincidunt felis. Aliquam bibendum,
> nibh ut commodo dignissim, turpis purus imperdiet lacus,
> faucibus convallis metus neque sit amet risus. Nulla
> pharetra dui vel suscipit pretium. Etiam a euismod ante.

Figure 13-4. The expanded details element

Discussion

By default, the inner content is hidden, and you'll just see a disclosure element with the contents of the `<summary>` element. In this case, the button will read More Info. When you click the More Info button, the hidden content will appear. If you click it again, the content again becomes hidden.

You can change this default behavior with the open attribute. If you add this attribute, the content will start out visible (see Example 13-12).

Example 13-12. Controlling the default state with the open attribute

```
<details open>
  <summary>More Info</summary>
  This content is visible by default.
</details>
```

Finally, you can also toggle the content with JavaScript. You can change the value of the element's open attribute directly, as shown in Example 13-13.

Example 13-13. Toggling the visibility with JavaScript

```
// Show the content
document.querySelector('details').open = true;
```

Most browsers have good accessibility support for this element, identifying the trigger element to screen readers and indicating its expanded or collapsed state.

13.5 Showing a Popover

Problem

You want to show pop-up content by clicking a button, but still allow the user to interact with the rest of the page.

Solution

Give the element a `popover` attribute, and add the `popovertarget` attribute to the trigger button (see Example 13-14).

Example 13-14. Automatically wiring a popover

```
<button type="button" popovertarget="greeting">Open Popover</button>
<div popover id="greeting">Hello world!</div>
```

 This API may not be supported by all browsers yet. See CanIUse (*https://oreil.ly/YFjQX*) for the latest compatibility data.

Discussion

A popover differs from a dialog in a few ways:

- You can open it without any JavaScript.
- There is no backdrop like there is with a dialog.
- Unlike a dialog, you aren't blocked from interacting with the underlying page while the popover is displayed.
- When you click outside of a popover, it will close.

To make an element into a popover, you give it the `popover` attribute. The popover element also needs an `id` attribute. To link a trigger button to the popover, the button is given a `popovertarget` attribute. The value of this attribute should correspond to the `id` of the popover.

One drawback of the popover API in its current state is that there is no mechanism to position the popover relative to its trigger. By default, the popover always appears centered on screen. If you want to change its position, you'll need to manually do that with CSS.

In the future, you will be able to use CSS anchor positioning to position the popover relative to its trigger. In the meantime, there are third-party libraries such as Floating UI that you can use to augment this solution in order to position the element.

13.6 Manually Controlling a Popover

Problem

You want to use the popover attribute but programmatically use JavaScript to have control over when the popover is shown and hidden.

Solution

Set the popover attribute to manual and call its showPopover, hidePopover, or togglePopover methods (see Example 13-15).

Example 13-15. The popover and trigger markup

```
<button type="button" id="trigger">Show Popover</button>
<div id="greeting" popover="manual">Hello World!</div>
```

 This API may not be supported by all browsers yet. See CanIUse (*https://oreil.ly/YFjQX*) for the latest compatibility data.

The popover="manual" attribute tells the browser that the popover will be manually controlled (see Example 13-16). To show the popover, select the popover element and call its togglePopover method. This will show the popover when it is hidden and hide the popover when it is shown.

Example 13-16. The toggle button code

```
const trigger = document.querySelector('#trigger');
const popover = document.querySelector('#greeting');
trigger.addEventListener('click', () => {
  popover.togglePopover();
});
```

Discussion

If you want to manually control the popover's visibility, make sure that you set the `popover` attribute to `manual`. When the popover element is set to manual control, clicking outside of the popover will *not* close it. To close the popover, you'll need to call either its `hidePopover` or `togglePopover` methods.

13.7 Positioning a Popover Relative to an Element

Problem

You want to show a popover, but you don't want it in the middle of the screen. You want to position it relative to another element, such as the button that triggered it.

Solution

Calculate the bounding rectangle of the element, then adjust the popover's position accordingly. This example will cover positioning the tooltip just below the element.

 This API may not be supported by all browsers yet. See CanIUse (*https://oreil.ly/YFjQX*) for the latest compatibility data.

First, you'll need to apply some styles to the popover element, as shown in Example 13-17.

Example 13-17. The popover styles

```
.popover {
  margin: 0;
  margin-top: 1em;
  position: absolute;
}
```

By default, the browser uses margin to center the popover within the viewport. To position the popover relative to another element, you need to remove this margin. Since you are positioning the tooltip below the other element, you can set a `margin-top` so that there's a small amount of space between the element and the popover. Finally, to make the popover scroll along with the element, you need to set `position: fixed`.

Next, you can use the `popovertarget` attribute on the trigger to automatically show the popover on click (see Example 13-18).

Example 13-18. The popover and trigger markup

```
<button type="button" class="trigger" popovertarget="popover">Show Popover</button>
<div class="popover" popover>
  This is popover content anchored to the trigger button.
</div>
```

The last step is to update the popover's position whenever it is shown. You can listen for the popover element's `toggle` event, which is triggered when the popover is either shown or hidden. When handling this event, you can calculate the trigger element's position and use it to update the popover's position (see Example 13-19).

Example 13-19. Setting the popover's position

```
const popover = document.querySelector('.popover');
const trigger = document.querySelector('.trigger');

popover.addEventListener('toggle', event => {
  // Update the position if the popover is being opened.
  if (event.newState === 'open') {
    // Find the position of the trigger element.
    const triggerRect = trigger.getBoundingClientRect();

    // Since the popover is positioned relative to the viewport,
    // you need to account for the scroll offset.
    popover.style.top = `${triggerRect.bottom + window.scrollY}px`;
    popover.style.left = `${triggerRect.left}px`;
  }
});
```

Discussion

If you are familiar with CSS positioning, you might be a little confused about the behavior of `position: absolute` here. Normally, `position: absolute` will position the element relative to its closest positioned ancestor element. In this case, though, the popover will always be positioned relative to the viewport.

This is because popovers are positioned inside the browser's *top layer*. This is a special layer that is on top of all other layers in the document. Regardless of where in the DOM your popover element exists, the popover content is placed in the top layer. Since it's in this special top layer, `position: absolute` will position the element relative to the viewport.

The position of the popover is calculated by calling `getBoundingClientRect` on the trigger element. As you scroll the page, the top and bottom positions of this rectangle will change. To make sure the popover is positioned correctly underneath the trigger, you also need to include `window.scrollY` in the calculation.

There are a few limitations to note of this implementation. First, if the trigger element is at the bottom of the document, there may not be enough room underneath the element to show the popover. You may want to check for this and, when there isn't enough room, position the popover *above* the trigger instead.

Another thing you might want to handle is if the window is resized while the popover is visible, the position may not be updated correctly. You could use a `ResizeObserver` or the window's `resize` event to handle this case.

13.8 Showing a Tooltip

Problem

You want to show a tooltip when hovering over, or focusing, an element.

Solution

Use a manually controlled popover, showing and hiding it with the corresponding mouse events. This will use the same positioning approach as in Recipe 13.7, so first you'll need to define the custom styles for the popover (see Example 13-20).

Example 13-20. The tooltip styles

```
#tooltip {
  margin: 0;
  margin-top: 1em;
  position: absolute;
}
```

> This API may not be supported by all browsers yet. See CanIUse (*https://oreil.ly/YFjQX*) for the latest compatibility data.

Implement the tooltip as a popover with the `popover` attribute set to `manual`, as shown in Example 13-21.

Example 13-21. The tooltip markup

```
<button type="button" id="trigger">Hover Me</button>
<div id="tooltip" popover="manual" role="tooltip">Here is some tooltip content</div>
```

When the mouse hovers over the trigger, calculate the position and show the popover element on the mouseover event. On the mouseout event, hide the popover element (see Example 13-22).

Example 13-22. Showing and hiding the tooltip

```
const button = document.querySelector('#trigger');
const tooltip = document.querySelector('#tooltip');

function showTooltip() {
  // Find the position of the trigger element.
  const triggerRect = trigger.getBoundingClientRect();

  // Since the popover is positioned relative to the viewport,
  // you need to account for the scroll offset.
  tooltip.style.top = `${triggerRect.bottom + window.scrollY}px`;
  tooltip.style.left = `${triggerRect.left}px`;

  tooltip.showPopover();
}

// Show and hide the tooltip in response to mouse events.
button.addEventListener('mouseover', () => {
  showTooltip();
});

button.addEventListener('mouseout', () => {
  tooltip.hidePopover();
});

// For keyboard accessibility, also show and hide the tooltip
// in response to focus events.
button.addEventListener('focus', () => {
  showTooltip();
});

button.addEventListener('blur', () => {
  tooltip.hidePopover();
});
```

Discussion

Since this uses the same positioning technique as Recipe 13.7, it has the same limitations:

- It doesn't account for the case where there's not enough room to show the tooltip below it.

- It doesn't account for resizing the window.

13.9 Showing a Notification

Problem

You want to notify the user when something occurs in your app.

Solution

Use a `Notification` object to show a native operating system notification.

In order to show notifications, you must first ask the user for permission. This is done with the `Notification.requestPermission` method. To check if the user has already given permission, you can check the `Notification.permission` property.

Notifications Versus Push Notifications

The notifications described in this recipe are only triggered when a user is on the page. This is different than push notifications, which can be delivered even when the page is not active. This is more involved, and it typically requires the use of a third-party service.

Example 13-23 shows a helper function that checks the permission, asks the user for permission if necessary, and returns a boolean indicating whether or not notifications can be shown.

Example 13-23. Checking notification permissions

```
async function getPermission() {
  // If the user has already explicitly denied permission, don't ask again.
  if (Notification.permission !== 'denied') {
    // The result of this permission request will update the Notification.permission
    // property.
    // The permission request returns a Promise.
    await Notification.requestPermission();
  }

  // Only show a notification if Notification.permission is 'granted'.
  return Notification.permission === 'granted';
}
```

Once you have checked for permission, you can send a new notification by creating a new `Notification` instance. Use the `getPermission` helper to determine if a notification should be shown (see Example 13-24).

Example 13-24. Showing a notification

```
if (await getPermission()) {
  new Notification('Hello!', {
    body: 'This is a test notification'
  });
}
```

If you try to show a notification when permission hasn't been granted, the Notifica
tion object will trigger an error event.

Figure 13-5 shows what this notification might look like on a desktop computer.

Figure 13-5. A notification rendered on macOS 14

Discussion

Notifications can only be shown from apps running in a *secure context*. Typically, this
means it must be served with HTTPS or from a localhost URL.

The Notification.permission property has one of three values:

granted
> The user has expressly granted permissions to show notifications.

denied
> The user has expressly denied permission to show notifications when prompted.

default
> The user hasn't responded to a notification permission request. Browsers will
> treat this the same as the denied case.

A Notification can trigger some other events as well:

show
> Triggered when the notification is shown

close
> Triggered when the notification closes

click
> Triggered when the notification is clicked

CHAPTER 14

Device Integration

14.0 Introduction

The modern web browser platform includes APIs to interact with all kinds of device information and capabilities, including:

- Battery status
- Network status
- Geolocation
- Device clipboard
- Sharing content
- Tactile feedback

At the time of writing, some of these APIs are not well supported yet. Some are still considered experimental, so you shouldn't use them in a production application just yet.

Some of these APIs may be supported by a given browser, like Chrome, but still won't work if the device is missing the required capabilities. For example, the Vibration API is well supported by Chrome, but won't work on a laptop or other device without vibration support.

14.1 Reading the Battery Status

Problem

You want to show the device's battery charging status in your app.

Solution

Use the Battery Status API.

 This API may not be supported by all browsers yet. See CanIUse (*https://oreil.ly/DWFvk*) for the latest compatibility data.

You can query the Battery Status API by calling `navigator.getBattery`. This method returns a `Promise` that resolves to an object containing battery information.

First, write some HTML placeholder elements to hold the battery status, as shown in Example 14-1.

Example 14-1. The battery status markup

```
<ul>
  <li>Battery charge level:<span id="battery-level">--</span></li>
  <li>Battery charge status:<span id="battery-charging">--</span></li>
</ul>
```

Then, you can query the Battery Status API to get the battery charge level and charging status, adding them to the corresponding DOM elements (see Example 14-2).

Example 14-2. Querying the Battery Status API

```
const batteryLevelItem = document.querySelector('#battery-level');
const batteryChargingItem = document.querySelector('#battery-charging');

navigator.getBattery().then(battery => {
  // Battery level is a number between 0 and 1. Multiply by 100 to convert it to
  // a percentage.
  batteryLevelItem.textContent = `${battery.level * 100}%`;

  batteryChargingItem.textContent = battery.charging ? 'Charging' : 'Not charging';
});
```

What if you unplug your laptop? The displayed charging status is no longer accurate. To handle this, there some events you can listen for:

levelchange
> Triggered when the battery's charge level changes

chargingchange
> Triggered when the battery starts or stops charging

You can update the UI when these events occur. Make sure you have a reference to the `battery` object, then add event listeners (see Example 14-3).

Example 14-3. Listening for battery events

```
battery.addEventListener('levelchange', () => {
  batteryLevelItem.textContent = `${battery.level * 100}%`;
});

battery.addEventListener('chargingchange', () => {
  batteryChargingItem.textContent = battery.charging ? 'Charging' : 'Not charging';
});
```

Now your battery status stays updated. If you unplug your laptop, the charging status changes from "Charging" to "Not charging."

Discussion

At the time of writing, some browsers don't support this API at all. You can use the code in Example 14-4 to check if the Battery Status API is supported on the user's browser.

Example 14-4. Checking for Battery Status API support

```
if ('getBattery' in navigator) {
  // request the battery status here
} else {
  // it's not supported
}
```

There are some additional properties available in the `battery` object, too. These include:

chargingTime
   The number of seconds remaining until the battery is fully charged, if the battery is charging. If the battery is not charging, this has the value `Infinity`.

dischargingTime
   The number of seconds remaining until the battery is fully discharged, if the battery is not charging. If the battery is not discharging, this has the value `Infinity`.

These two properties also have their own `change` events that you can listen for, called `chargingtimechange` and `dischargingtimechange`, respectively.

There are many things you can do with the information provided by the Battery Status API. For example, if the battery level is low, you can disable background tasks or other power-intensive operations. Or, it could even be something as simple as letting the user know they should save their changes because the device's battery level is low.

You could also use it to show a simple battery status indicator. If you have a series of icons representing different battery states (fully charged, not charging, charging, low charge) you could keep the displayed icon up to date by listening to the change events.

14.2 Reading the Network Status

Problem

You want to know how fast the user's network connection is.

Solution

Use the Network Information API to get data about the user's network connection (see Example 14-5).

Example 14-5. Checking the network capabilities

```
if (navigator.connection.effectiveType === '4g') {
  // User can perform high-bandwidth activities.
}
```

 This API may not be supported by all browsers yet. See CanIUse (*https://oreil.ly/krDAV*) for the latest compatibility data.

Discussion

The network information is contained in the `navigator.connection` object. To get an approximation of the network connection capabilities, you can check the `navigator.connection.effectiveType` property. At the time of writing, the possible values for `navigator.connection.effectiveType` based on download speed are:

- `slow-2g`: Up to 50 Kbps
- `2g`: Up to 70 Kbps
- `3g`: Up to 700 Kbps
- `4g`: 700 Kbps and above

These values are calculated based on the measurement of real user data. The specification states that these values may be updated in the future. You can use these values to determine, approximately, the network capabilities of the device. For example, an effectiveType of slow-2g probably cannot handle high-bandwidth activities like HD video streaming.

Should the network connection change while the page is open, the navigator.con nection object can trigger a change event. You can listen for this event and adjust your app based on the new network connection information that was received.

14.3 Getting the Device Location

Problem

You want to get the device's location.

Solution

Use the Geolocation API to get the position in latitude and longitude. The Geolocation API exposes the navigator.geolocation object, which is used to request the user's location with the getCurrentPosition method. This is a callback-based API. getCurrentPosition takes two arguments. The first argument is the success callback, and the second is the error callback (see Example 14-6).

Example 14-6. Requesting the device location

```
navigator.geolocation.getCurrentPosition(position => {
  console.log('Latitude: ' + position.coords.latitude);
  console.log('Longitude: ' + position.coords.longitude);
}, error => {
  // Either the user denied permission, or the device location could not
  // be determined.
  console.log(error);
});
```

This API requires permission from the user. The first time you call getCurrentPosi tion, the browser asks the user for permission to share their location. If the user does not grant permission, the geolocation request fails and the browser calls the error callback.

If you want to check for permission ahead of time, to avoid having to catch an error, you can use the Permissions API to check its status (see Example 14-7).

Example 14-7. Checking for geolocation permission

```
const permission = await navigator.permissions.query({
  name: 'geolocation'
});
```

The returned permission object has a `state` property that can have one of the values `granted`, `denied`, or `prompt`. If the state is `denied`, you know the user has already been prompted and they declined, so you shouldn't bother trying to get their location because it will fail.

Discussion

There are a few ways the browser can try to detect a user's location. It can attempt to use the device's GPS, or it may use information about the user's WiFi connection or IP address. In some cases, such as when the user is using a VPN, IP-based geolocation may not return the correct location for the user's device.

The Geolocation API has very good browser support, so you don't need to check for feature support unless you are targeting old browsers.

In addition to the coordinates, the `position` object contains some other interesting information that may not be available on all devices:

`altitude`
　　The device's altitude above sea level, in meters

`heading`
　　The device's compass heading, in degrees

`speed`
　　The velocity of the device, if it is moving, in meters per second

You can also watch for changes in the device's location by calling `navigator.geoloca` `tion.watchCurrentPosition`. The browser calls the callback that you pass to this method periodically when the location changes, providing updated coordinates.

Geolocation Versus Geocoding

The Geolocation API can only get the device's coordinates (latitude and longitude). It can't determine the state, city, or specific address you are at. For this, you need a *geocoding* API, which is not built into the browser. There are many external geocoding APIs available from vendors such as Microsoft and Google. Geocoding is the process of taking an address and converting it to latitude and longitude. Some of these services can also do *reverse geocoding*, which takes latitude and longitude coordinates and converts them into an address.

14.4 Showing the Device Location on a Map

Problem

You want to show a map of the device's location.

Solution

Use a service like Google Maps API or OpenStreetMaps to generate a map, passing the latitude and longitude coordinates from the Geolocation API.

 For this recipe, you need to sign up for a Google Maps API key. You can find instructions to sign up for an API key on the Google Developers website (*https://oreil.ly/9Uujk*).

This example shows how to embed a map with the Google Maps Embed API. You can use the Google Maps Embed API by embedding an `iframe` element with a specially crafted URL. The URL must contain:

- The type of map (for this example, you need a `place` map)
- Your API key
- The geolocation coordinates

Request the device location, and in the success callback you can create the `iframe` and add it to the document (see Example 14-8.

Example 14-8. Creating a map iframe

```
// Assuming you have a placeholder element in the page with the ID 'map'
const map = document.querySelector('#map');

navigator.geolocation.getCurrentPosition(position => {
  const { latitude, longitude } = position.coords;

  // Adjust the iframe size as desired.
  const iframe = document.createElement('iframe');
  iframe.width = 450;
  iframe.height = 250;

  // The map type is part of the URL path.
  const url = new URL('https://www.google.com/maps/embed/v1/place');

  // The 'key' parameter contains your API key.
  url.searchParams.append('key', 'YOUR_GOOGLE_MAPS_API_KEY');
```

```
// The 'q' parameter contains the latitude and longitude coordinates
// separated by a comma.
url.searchParams.append('q', `${latitude},${longitude}`);
iframe.src = url;

  map.appendChild(iframe);
});
```

Discussion

See this article from Google (*https://oreil.ly/WhO-r*) to learn more about properly securing a Google Maps API key.

This is just one of many possible map integrations you can use once you have received the device's location. Google Maps has other types of APIs, and there are other services such as Mapbox or OpenStreetMap. You can also integrate a geocoding API to show a map marker with the actual address.

14.5 Copying and Pasting Text

Problem

Within a text area, you want to add copy and paste functionality. The user should be able to highlight some text and copy it, and when pasting, it should replace whatever text is selected.

Solution

Use the Clipboard API to interact with the selected text within the text area. You can add Copy and Paste buttons to your UI that call the corresponding functionality in the Clipboard API.

> This API may not be fully supported by all browsers yet. See Can-IUse (*https://oreil.ly/4i7sm*) for the latest compatibility data.

To copy the text, get the selection start and end indexes and take that substring of the text area's value. Then, write that text to the system clipboard (see Example 14-9).

Example 14-9. Copying text from a selection

```
async function copySelection(textarea) {
  const { selectionStart, selectionEnd } = textarea;
```

```
  const selectedText = textarea.value.slice(selectionStart, selectionEnd);

  try {
    await navigator.clipboard.writeText(selectedText);
  } catch (error) {
    console.error('Clipboard error:', error);
  }
}
```

Pasting is similar, but there's an extra step. If there is text selected within the text area, you need to remove the selected text and splice in the new text from the clipboard (see Example 14-10). The Clipboard API is asynchronous, so you'll need to wait on a Promise to receive the value in the system clipboard.

Example 14-10. Pasting text into a selection

```
async function pasteToSelection(textarea) {
  const currentValue = textarea.value;
  const { selectionStart, selectionEnd } = textarea;

  try {
    const clipboardValue = await navigator.clipboard.readText();
    const newValue = currentValue.slice(0, selectionStart)
    + clipboardValue + currentValue.slice(selectionEnd);
    textarea.value = newValue;
  } catch (error) {
    console.error('Clipboard error:', error);
  }
}
```

This replaces the currently selected text with the text from the clipboard.

Discussion

Note that even though you aren't doing anything with the return value of naviga tor.clipboard.writeText, you are still awaiting the Promise. This is because you need to handle the case when the Promise is rejected with an error.

Also, when pasting, there are two other scenarios to be aware of:

- If no text is selected but the text area has focus, the text is pasted at the cursor position.
- If the text area does not have focus, the text is pasted at the end of the text area's value.

As you might expect, reading from the system clipboard programmatically can be a privacy concern. As such, it requires user permission. The first time you try to read from the clipboard, the browser asks the user for permission. If they allow it, the clipboard operation completes. If they deny the permission, the `Promise` returned by the Clipboard API is rejected with an error.

If you want to avoid permission errors, you can use the Permissions API to check if the user has granted permission to read from the system clipboard (see Example 14-11).

Example 14-11. Checking clipboard read permission

```
const permission = await navigator.permissions.query({
  name: 'clipboard-read'
});

if (permission.state !== 'denied') {
  // Continue with the clipboard read operation.
}
```

The three possible values for `permission.state` are:

granted
> The user has already explicitly granted permission.

denied
> The user has already explicitly denied permission.

prompt
> The user has not been asked for permission yet.

If `permission.state` has the value `prompt`, the browser automatically prompts the user the first time you attempt to perform a clipboard read operation.

14.6 Sharing Content with the Web Share API

Problem

You want to give the user an easy way to share a link using the native sharing capabilities of their device.

Solution

Use the Web Share API to share the content.

This API may not be supported by all browsers yet. See CanIUse (*https://oreil.ly/1IwEq*) for the latest compatibility data.

Call `navigator.share` and pass an object containing the title and URL (see Example 14-12). On supported devices and browsers, this brings up a familiar sharing interface that allows them to share the link in various ways.

Example 14-12. Sharing a link

```
if ('share' in navigator) {
  navigator.share({
    title: 'Web API Cookbook',
    text: 'Check out this awesome site!',
    url: 'https://browserapis.dev'
  });
}
```

From here, the user can create a text message, email, or other communication containing a link to the content.

Discussion

The sharing interface looks different depending on the device and operating system. For example, Figure 14-1 is a screenshot of the sharing interface on my computer running macOS 14.

Figure 14-1. The share interface on macOS 14

14.7 Making the Device Vibrate

Problem

You want to add some tactile feedback to your app, making the user's device vibrate.

Solution

Use the Vibration API to programmatically vibrate the device.

This API may not be supported by all browsers yet. See CanIUse (*https://oreil.ly/G0d6m*) for the latest compatibility data.

To perform a single vibration, you can call `navigator.vibrate` with a single integer argument (the duration of the vibration), as shown in Example 14-13.

Example 14-13. Triggering a single vibration

```
// A single vibration for 500ms
navigator.vibrate(500);
```

You can also trigger a sequence of vibrations by passing an array to `naviga tor.vibrate` (see Example 14-14). The elements of the array are interpreted as a sequence of vibrations and pauses.

Example 14-14. Vibrating three times

```
// Vibrate for 500ms three times, with a 250ms pause in between
navigator.vibrate([500, 250, 500, 250, 500]);
```

Discussion

This API is supported on some devices that don't vibrate, for example Chrome on a MacBook Pro. For these devices, calling `navigator.vibrate` has no effect, but it also won't throw any error.

If a sequence of vibrations is running, you can call `navigator.vibrate(0)` to cancel any in-progress vibrations.

Like autoplaying videos, you can't trigger vibration automatically when the page first loads. The user must have interacted with the page in some way before vibration can be done.

14.8 Getting the Device Orientation

Problem

You want to determine if the device is in portrait or landscape orientation.

Solution

Use the `screen.orientation.type` property to get the device orientation, or use the `screen.orientation.angle` property to get the device's orientation angle relative to its natural orientation.

Discussion

`screen.orientation.type` can have one of four values, depending on the device and its orientation (see Figure 14-2):

- `portrait-primary`: 0 degrees (the natural device position)
- `portrait-secondary`: 180 degrees
- `landscape-primary`: 90 degrees
- `landscape-secondary`: 270 degrees

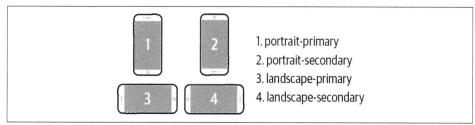

Figure 14-2. The different orientation values

The preceding values are for devices such as phones, whose natural orientation is portrait. For other devices whose natural orientation is landscape, like some tablets, the values are reversed:

- `landscape-primary`: 0 degrees (the natural device position)
- `landscape-secondary`: 180 degrees
- `portrait-primary`: 90 degrees
- `portrait-secondary`: 270 degrees

The `screen.orientation` object also has a `change` event you can listen for to be notified of changes in the device orientation.

CHAPTER 15

Measuring Performance

15.0 Introduction

There are many third-party tools for measuring performance in a JavaScript app, but the browser also has some handy tools built in for capturing performance metrics.

The Navigation Timing API is used to capture performance data about the initial page load. You can inspect how long the page took to load, how long it took for the DOM to become interactive, and more. It returns a set of timestamps that indicate when each event happened during the page load.

The Resource Timing API lets you inspect how long it took to download resources and make network requests. This covers page resources such as HTML files, CSS files, JavaScript files, and images. It also covers asynchronous requests such as those made with the Fetch API.

The User Timing API is a way to calculate the elapsed time of arbitrary operations. You can create performance *marks*, which are points in time, and *measures*, which are calculated durations between marks.

All of these APIs create performance entries in a buffer on the page. This is a single collection of all types of performance entries. You can inspect this buffer at any time, and you can also use `PerformanceObserver` to listen asynchronously for new performance entries to be added.

Performance entries use high-precision timestamps. Time is measured in milliseconds, but can also contain fractional portions that, in some browsers, can have microsecond accuracy. In the browser, these timestamps are stored as `DOMHighResTimeStamp` objects. These are numbers that start at zero when the page loads and represent the time since the page load that a given entry happened.

This chapter's recipes explore solutions for gathering performance metrics. What you do with those metrics is up to you. You can use the Fetch or Beacon API to send the performance metrics to an API for collection and later analysis.

You can use these performance metrics during development for debugging purposes, or leave them in to collect real performance metrics from your users. These can be sent to an analytics service for aggregation and analysis.

15.1 Measuring Page Load Performance

Problem

You want to gather information about the timing of page load events.

Solution

Look up the single performance entry with a type of `navigation`, and retrieve the navigation timestamps from the performance entry object (see Example 15-1). You can then calculate the interval between these timestamps to figure out the time taken for various page load events.

Example 15-1. Looking up the navigation timing performance entry

```
// There is only one navigation performance entry.
const [navigation] = window.performance.getEntriesByType('navigation');
```

This object has a lot of properties. Table 15-1 lists a few examples of useful calculations you can perform.

Table 15-1. Navigation timing calculations

Metric	Start time	End time
Time to first byte	startTime	responseStart
Time to DOM interactive	startTime	domInteractive
Total load time	startTime	loadEventEnd

Discussion

The `startTime` property of the navigation timing performance entry is always 0.

This entry doesn't only contain timing information. It also contains information such as the amount of data transferred, the HTTP response code, and the page URL. This information is useful to determine how quickly your application becomes responsive when it first loads.

15.2 Measuring Resource Performance

Problem

You want to get information about requests for the resources loaded on the page.

Solution

Find the resource performance entries in the performance buffer (see Example 15-2).

Example 15-2. Getting the resource performance entries

```
const entries = window.performance.getEntriesByType('resource');
```

You'll get one entry for each resource on the page. Resources include CSS files, Java-Script files, images, and any other requests by the page.

For each resource, you can calculate how long it took to load by taking the difference between the `startTime` and `responseEnd` properties. The URL of the resource is available in the `name` property.

Discussion

Any network requests you make with the Fetch API also show up as a resource. This makes this API useful for profiling the real-world performance of your REST API endpoints.

When the page first loads, the performance buffer includes an entry for all resources requested during the initial page load. Subsequent requests are added to the performance buffer as they are made.

15.3 Finding the Slowest Resources

Problem

You want to get a list of the resources that took the longest to load.

Solution

Sort and filter the list of resource performance entries. Since this list is just an array, you can call methods such as `sort` and `slice` on it. To find how long the resource took to load, take the difference between its `responseEnd` and `startTime` timestamps.

Example 15-3 shows how to find the five slowest-loading resources.

Example 15-3. Finding the five slowest-loading resources

```
const slowestResources = window.performance.getEntriesByType('resource')
  .sort((a, b) =>
    (b.responseEnd - b.startTime) - (a.responseEnd - a.startTime))
  .slice(0, 5);
```

Discussion

The key is the `sort` call. This compares each pair of load times and sorts the whole list in descending order of load times. Then, the `slice` call is just taking the first five elements of the sorted array.

If you want to instead get a list of the five fastest-loading resources, you can just reverse the order in which the load times are compared (see Example 15-4).

Example 15-4. Finding the 5 fastest resources

```
const fastestResources = window.performance.getEntriesByType('resource')
  .sort((a, b) =>
    (a.responseEnd - a.startTime) - (b.responseEnd - b.startTime))
  .slice(0, 5);
```

The reversed comparison means the array is sorted in ascending order rather than descending order. The `slice` call now returns the five fastest-loading resources.

15.4 Finding Timings for a Specific Resource

Problem

You want to look up the timings for requests for a specific resource.

Solution

Use the method `window.performance.getEntriesByName` to look up resources by a specific URL (see Example 15-5).

Example 15-5. Finding all resource timings for a specific URL

```
// Look up all requests to the /api/users API
const entries = window.performance.getEntriesByName('https://localhost/api/users',
  'resource');
```

Discussion

The name of a resource entry is its URL. The first argument to `getEntriesByName` is the URL. The second argument indicates that you're interested in resource timings.

If there were multiple requests for the given URL, you'll get multiple resource entries in the returned array.

15.5 Profiling Rendering Performance

Problem

You want to record the time it takes to render some data on the page.

Solution

Create a performance mark just before the rendering begins. Once rendering is complete, create another mark. Then you can create a *measure* between the two marks to record how long the rendering took.

Imagine you have a `DataView` component that can be used to render some data in the page (see Example 15-6).

Example 15-6. Measuring rendering performance

```
// Create the initial performance mark just before rendering.
window.performance.mark('render-start');

// Create the component and render the data.
const dataView = new DataView();
dataView.render(data);

// When rendering is done, create the ending performance mark.
window.performance.mark('render-end');

// Create a measure between the two marks.
const measure = window.performance.measure('render', 'render-start', 'render-end');
```

The `measure` object contains the start time and the calculated duration of the measure.

Discussion

Whenever you create performance marks and measures, they are added to the page's performance buffer to look up later. For example, if you wanted to look up the `render` measure at a later time, you could use `window.performance.getEntriesByName` (see Example 15-7).

Example 15-7. Looking up a measure by name

```
// There is only one 'render' measure, so you can use
// array destructuring to get the first (and only) entry.
const [renderMeasure] = window.performance.getEntriesByName('render');
```

Marks and measures can also contain data associated with them by passing the `detail` option. For example, when rendering the data in Example 15-6, you can pass the data itself as metadata when creating the measure.

When creating a measure in this way, you need to include the start and end marks inside the options object (see Example 15-8).

Example 15-8. Measuring rendering performance with data

```
// Create the initial performance mark just before rendering.
window.performance.mark('render-start');

// Create the component and render the data.
const dataView = new DataView();
dataView.render(data);

// When rendering is done, create the ending performance mark.
window.performance.mark('render-end');

// Create a measure between the two marks, passing the
// data being rendered as the measure detail.
const measure = window.performance.measure('render', {
  start: 'render-start',
  end: 'render-end',
  detail: data
});
```

Later, when you look up this performance entry, the detail metadata is available in the measure's `detail` property.

15.6 Profiling Multistep Tasks

Problem

You want to gather performance data for a multistep process. You want to get the time for the whole sequence, but also the time for individual steps. For example, you might want to load some data from an API and then do some processing with that data. In this case, you want to know the time for the API request, the time for the processing, and also the total time taken.

Solution

Create multiple marks and measures. You can use a given mark in more than one measure calculation.

In Example 15-9, there's an API that returns some user transactions. Once the transactions are received, you want to run some analytics on the transaction data. Finally, the analytics data is sent to another API.

Example 15-9. Profiling a multistep process

```
window.performance.mark('transactions-start');
const transactions = await fetch('/api/users/123/transactions');
window.performance.mark('transactions-end');
window.performance.mark('process-start');
const analytics = processAnalytics(transactions);
window.performance.mark('process-end');
window.performance.mark('upload-start');
await fetch('/api/analytics', {
  method: 'POST',
  body: JSON.stringify(analytics),
  headers: {
    'Content-Type': 'application/json'
  }
});
window.performance.mark('upload-end');
```

Once the process has finished and marks have been taken, you can use those marks to generate several measures, as shown in Example 15-10.

Example 15-10. Generating measures

```
console.log('Download transactions:',
  window.performance.measure(
    'transactions', 'transactions-start', 'transactions-end'
  ).duration
);

console.log('Process analytics:',
  window.performance.measure(
    'analytics', 'process-start', 'process-end'
  ).duration
);

console.log('Upload analytics:',
  window.performance.measure(
    'upload', 'upload-start', 'upload-end'
  ).duration
);
```

```
console.log('Total time:',
  window.performance.measure(
    'total', 'transactions-start', 'upload-end'
  ).duration
);
```

Discussion

This example shows how you can create multiple marks and measures to gather per-formance data on a set of tasks. A given mark can be used more than once, in multiple measures. Example 15-10 creates a measure for each step of the process, then generates a final measure for the entire task's duration. This is done by taking the first mark of the download task and the last mark of the upload task, and calculating a measure between them.

15.7 Listening for Performance Entries

Problem

You want to be notified of new performance entries so that you can report them to an analytics service. For example, consider the scenario where you want to be notified of performance statistics every time an API request is made.

Solution

Use a `PerformanceObserver` to listen for new performance entries of the desired type. For API requests, the type would be `resource` (see Example 15-11).

Example 15-11. Using a `PerformanceObserver`

```
const analyticsEndpoint = 'https://example.com/api/analytics';

const observer = new PerformanceObserver(entries => {
  for (let entry of entries.getEntries()) {
    // Only interested in 'fetch' entries.
    // Use the Beacon API to send a quick request containing the performance
    // entry data.
    if (entry.initiatorType === 'fetch') {
      navigator.sendBeacon(analyticsEndpoint, entry);
    }
  }
});

observer.observe({ type: 'resource' });
```

Discussion

The `PerformanceObserver` fires for every network request, including the one you make to your analytics service. For this reason, Example 15-11 checks to make sure a given entry is not the analytics endpoint before sending the request. Without this check, you end up in an infinite loop of POST requests. When a network request is made, the observer fires and you send the POST request. This creates a new performance entry, which calls the observer again. Each POST to the analytics service triggers a new observer callback.

To prevent a high volume of requests in a short period to your analytics service, for a real application you may want to collect performance entries in a buffer. Once the buffer reaches a certain size, you can send all the entries from the buffer in a single request (see Example 15-12).

Example 15-12. Sending performance entries in batches

```
const analyticsEndpoint = 'https://example.com/api/analytics';

// An array to hold buffered entries. Once the buffer reaches the desired size,
// all entries are sent in a single request.
const BUFFER_SIZE = 10;
let buffer = [];

const observer = new PerformanceObserver(entries => {
  for (let entry of entries.getEntries()) {
    if (entry.initiatorType === 'fetch' && entry.name !== analyticsEndpoint) {
      buffer.push(entry);
    }

    // If the buffer has reached its target size, send the analytics request.
    if (buffer.length === BUFFER_SIZE) {
      fetch(analyticsEndpoint, {
        method: 'POST',
        body: JSON.stringify(buffer),
        headers: {
          'Content-Type': 'application/json'
        }
      });

      // Reset the buffer now that the batched entries have been sent.
      buffer = [];
    }
  }
});

observer.observe({ type: 'resource' });
```

CHAPTER 16

Working with the Console

16.0 Introduction

Despite your best intentions, things can and will go wrong with your code. There are several debugging tools available to you. Today's browsers have powerful debuggers built in to them that let you step through code and inspect the values of variables and expressions. Sometimes, though, you might want to keep it simple and use the console.

In its most basic form, you interact with the console by calling `console.log` with a message. This message is printed to the browser's JavaScript console. While more verbose than breakpoint-based debugging, sometimes it can still be useful to log and inspect values at runtime.

Other than a simple `console.log`, there are other things you can do with the console such as group messages, use counters, display tables, and even style your output with CSS. There are also other log levels (error, warn, debug) that you can use to categorize and filter your console messages.

16.1 Styling Console Output

Problem

You want to apply some CSS to your console log output. For example, maybe you want to make the font larger and change the color.

Solution

Use the %c *directive* in your log message to denote what text you want styled. For each usage of %c, add another argument to console.log containing CSS styles (see Example 16-1).

Example 16-1. Styling console output

```
console.log('%cHello world!', 'font-size: 2rem; color: red;');
console.log('This console message uses %cstyled text. %cCool!',
  'font-style: italic;',
  'font-weight: bold;'
);
```

Figure 16-1 shows what this styled text looks like in the console.

Figure 16-1. The styled console output

Discussion

console.log takes a variable number of arguments. For each use of the %c directive, there should be a corresponding extra argument containing the styles to apply for that section of text.

Notice in Figure 16-1 that the styles are reset between each %c section. The italic font from the first section does not carry over into the bold font from the second section.

16.2 Using Log Levels

Problem

You want to distinguish between informational, warning, and error messages in the console.

Solution

Instead of console.log, use console.info, console.warn, and console.error, respectively (see Example 16-2). These messages are styled differently, and most browsers allow you to filter log messages by their level.

Example 16-2. Using different log levels

```
console.info('This is an info message');
console.warn('This is a warning message');
console.error('This is an error message');
```

The messages are styled differently, with icons, as shown in Figure 16-2.

```
                 This is a log message
        ⚠ ▸ This is a warning message
        ⊗ ▸ This is an error message
```

Figure 16-2. The different log levels (shown in Chrome)

Discussion

Warning and error messages also present you with a stack trace that can be expanded and viewed in the console. This makes it easy to track down where an error occurred.

16.3 Creating Named Loggers

Problem

You want to log messages from different modules of your app, prefixed with the module name in a given color.

Solution

Use `Function.prototype.bind` on the `console.log` function, binding the module name prefix and color style (see Example 16-3).

Example 16-3. Creating a named logger

```
function createLogger(name, color) {
  return console.log.bind(console, `%c${name}`, `color: ${color};`);
}
```

The `createLogger` function returns a new log function that you can call just like con sole.log, but messages have a colored prefix (see Example 16-4).

Example 16-4. Using the named loggers

```
const rendererLogger = createLogger('renderer', 'blue');
const dataLogger = createLogger('data', 'green');
```

```
// Outputs with a blue "renderer" prefix
rendererLogger('Rendering component');

// Outputs with a green "data" prefix
dataLogger('Fetching data');
```

This renders log messages with colored prefixes, as shown in Figure 16-3.

```
renderer Rendering component
data Fetching data
```

Figure 16-3. Colored loggers (shown in Chrome)

Discussion

Calling bind in this way creates a *partially applied* version of the console.log function that automatically adds the prefix and color. Any further arguments you pass to it are added after the prefix and color style.

16.4 Displaying an Array of Objects in a Table

Problem

You have an array of objects that you want to log in an easily readable way.

Solution

Pass the array to console.table and it displays a table. There is a column for each object property, and a row for each object in the array (see Example 16-5).

Example 16-5. Logging a table

```
const users = [
  { firstName: "John", lastName: "Smith", department: "Sales" },
  { firstName: "Emily", lastName: "Johnson", department: "Marketing" },
  { firstName: "Michael", lastName: "Davis", department: "Human Resources" },
  { firstName: "Sarah", lastName: "Thompson", department: "Finance" },
  { firstName: "David", lastName: "Wilson", department: "Engineering" }
];

console.table(users);
```

Figure 16-4 shows how the data is logged in table form.

(index)	firstName	lastName	department
0	'John'	'Smith'	'Sales'
1	'Emily'	'Johnson'	'Marketing'
2	'Michael'	'Davis'	'Human Resources'
3	'Sarah'	'Thompson'	'Finance'
4	'David'	'Wilson'	'Engineering'

Figure 16-4. The logged table (shown in Chrome)

Discussion

You can limit what object properties are shown by passing a second argument to `con sole.table`. This argument is an array of property names. If given, only those properties are shown in the table output.

`console.table` can also be used with an object. In Example 16-6, the `index` column contains the property names rather than array indices.

Example 16-6. Passing an object to `console.table`

```
console.table({
  name: 'sysadmin',
  email: 'admin@example.com'
});
```

Example 16-6 produces the table in Figure 16-5.

(index)	Value
name	'sysadmin'
email	'admin@example.com'

Figure 16-5. The logged table (shown in Chrome)

Example 16-7 logs the users in a table, but only shows the firstName and lastName columns (see Figure 16-6).

Example 16-7. Limiting table columns

```
const users = [
  { firstName: "John", lastName: "Smith", department: "Sales" },
  { firstName: "Emily", lastName: "Johnson", department: "Marketing" },
  { firstName: "Michael", lastName: "Davis", department: "Human Resources" },
  { firstName: "Sarah", lastName: "Thompson", department: "Finance" },
```

```
  { firstName: "David", lastName: "Wilson", department: "Engineering" }
];

console.table(users, ['firstName', 'lastName']);
```

(index)	firstName	lastName
0	'John'	'Smith'
1	'Emily'	'Johnson'
2	'Michael'	'Davis'
3	'Sarah'	'Thompson'
4	'David'	'Wilson'

Figure 16-6. Showing only the first and last name columns (shown in Chrome)

The rendered table is also sortable. You can click on a column name to sort the table by that column (see Figure 16-7).

(index)	firstName	lastName
2	'Michael'	'Davis'
1	'Emily'	'Johnson'
0	'John'	'Smith'
3	'Sarah'	'Thompson'
4	'David'	'Wilson'

Figure 16-7. Sorting the table by last name (shown in Chrome)

16.5 Using Console Timers

Problem

You want to calculate the time taken by some code, for debugging purposes.

Solution

Use the console.time and console.timeEnd methods (see Example 16-8).

Example 16-8. Using console.time and console.timeEnd

```
// Start the' loadTransactions' timer.
console.time('loadTransactions');

// Load some data.
const data = await fetch('/api/users/123/transactions');
```

```
// Stop the 'loadTransactions' timer.
// Prints: "loadTransactions: <elapsed time> ms"
console.timeEnd('loadTransactions');
```

When you call `console.time` with a timer name, it starts the named timer. Go perform whatever work you want to profile and when you're done, call `console.timeEnd` with the same timer name. The elapsed time, along with the timer name, is printed to the console.

If you call `console.timeEnd` with a timer name that doesn't match a previous call to `console.time`, no error is thrown, but a warning message is logged to the console that the timer does not exist.

Discussion

This is different from using `window.performance.mark` and `window.performance` `.measure` as described in Chapter 15. `console.time` is used for ad hoc timing, usually during debugging. The notable difference is that `console.time` and `console.time` End do *not* add entries to the performance timeline. Once you call `console.timeEnd` for a given timer, that timer is destroyed. If you want timing data that is persisted in memory, you might want to use the Performance API instead.

16.6 Using Console Groups

Problem

You want to better organize groups of log messages.

Solution

Use `console.group` to create nested groups of messages that can be expanded and collapsed (see Example 16-9).

Example 16-9. Using console groups

```
const users = [
  { id: 1, firstName: "John", lastName: "Smith", department: "Sales" },
  { id: 2, firstName: "Emily", lastName: "Johnson", department: "Marketing" },
  { id: 3, firstName: "Michael", lastName: "Davis", department: "Human Resources" },
  { id: 4, firstName: "Sarah", lastName: "Thompson", department: "Finance" },
  { id: 5, firstName: "David", lastName: "Wilson", department: "Engineering" }
];

console.log('Updating user data');
for (const user of users) {
```

```
  console.group(`User: ${user.firstName} ${user.lastName}`);
  console.log('Loading employee data from API');
  const response = await fetch(`/api/users/${user.id}`);
  const userData = await response.json();

  console.log('Updating profile');
  userData.lastUpdated = Date.now();

  console.log('Saving user data');
  await fetch(`/api/users/${user.id}`, {
    method: 'POST',
    body: JSON.stringify(userData),
    headers: {
      'Content-Type': 'application/json'
    }
  });
  console.groupEnd();
}
```

This prints grouped messages to the console. You can expand and collapse the groups so you can focus on the specific group you're interested in, as shown in Figure 16-8.

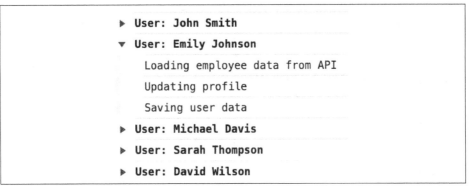

Figure 16-8. *Grouped console messages (shown in Chrome)*

Discussion

You can also use console groups to trace complex algorithms. Groups can be nested several levels deep, making it much easier to follow your log messages during a complex calculation. This is particularly valuable when there are a lot of messages to sort through. If you want a group to be collapsed by default, you can call `console.group Collapsed` instead of `console.group`.

16.7 Using Counters

Problem

You want to count the number of times a part of your code is called.

Solution

Call `console.count` with a counter name that is unique to your code. Every time the `console.count` statement is executed, it prints and increments the counter value. This lets you keep track of how many times the call to `console.count` was hit.

Example 16-10. Using counters

```
const users = [
  { id: 1, firstName: "John", lastName: "Smith", department: "Sales" },
  { id: 2, firstName: "Emily", lastName: "Johnson", department: "Marketing" },
  { id: 3, firstName: "Michael", lastName: "Davis", department: "Human Resources" },
  { id: 4, firstName: "Sarah", lastName: "Thompson", department: "Finance" },
  { id: 5, firstName: "David", lastName: "Wilson", department: "Engineering" }
];

users.forEach(user => {
  console.count('user');
});
```

Example 16-10 prints out the output shown in Example 16-11.

Example 16-11. The counter output

```
user: 1
user: 2
user: 3
user: 4
user: 5
```

Discussion

`console.count` is useful for tracing loop iterations or recursive function calls. Like other console methods, it is primarily intended for debugging purposes and isn't meant for collecting usage metrics.

You can also call `console.count` without any arguments, in which case it uses a counter called `default`.

16.8 Logging a Variable and Its Value

Problem

You want to log a variable name and its value without having to type the name twice.

Solution

Use object shorthand notation to log an object containing the variable (see Example 16-12).

Example 16-12. Logging a variable and its value

```
const username = 'sysadmin';

// logs { username: 'sysadmin' }
console.log({ username });
```

This creates an object whose name is `username`, and whose value is the value of the `username` variable, and logs it to the console, as shown in Figure 16-9.

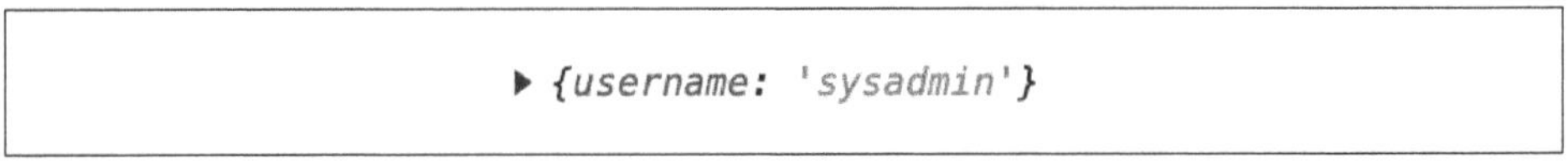

> ▶ *{username: 'sysadmin'}*

Figure 16-9. Object with the named value (shown in Chrome)

Discussion

Before object shorthand notation, you would need to type the variable name twice (see Example 16-13).

Example 16-13. Logging a variable and its value without object shorthand

```
const username = 'sysadmin';

console.log('username', username);
```

It's not much of a change, but it's a quick time-saving shortcut.

16.9 Logging a Stack Trace

Problem

You want to see a stack trace of where the code is currently being executed.

Solution

Use `console.trace` to log a trace of the current call stack (see Example 16-14).

Example 16-14. Using `console.trace`

```
function foo() {
  function bar() {
    console.trace();
  }
  bar();
}

foo();
```

This outputs the stack trace shown in Figure 16-10.

```
▼ console.trace
  bar                            @ VM3574:5
  foo                            @ VM3574:7
  (anonymous)                    @ VM3574:10
```

Figure 16-10. Logging a stack trace (shown in Chrome)

Discussion

A stack trace is a useful debugging tool. It shows the current state of the call stack. The first entry in the stack trace is the `console.trace` call itself. Then, the next entry is whatever function called the function containing the `console.trace` call, and so on. In most browsers, you can click on a stack trace element to jump to that line of code. You can use this to add log statements or set breakpoints.

16.10 Validating Expected Values

Problem

While debugging, you want to make sure an expression has an expected value. If it doesn't, you want to see a console error.

Solution

Use `console.assert` to print an error if the expression doesn't match what you expect (see Example 16-15).

Example 16-15. Using `console.assert`

```
function updateUser(user) {
  // Log an error if the user id is null.
  console.assert(user.id !== null, 'user.id must not be null');

  // Update the user.
  return fetch(`/api/users/${user.id}`, {
    method: 'PUT',
    body: JSON.stringify(user),
    headers: {
      'Content-Type': 'application/json'
    }
  });
}
```

If `updateUser` is called with a user object without an `id` property, the error is logged.

Discussion

Assertions are not typically used in production, as it's a debugging tool like the other console methods. It's important to note that if an assertion fails, it prints an error but does not throw an error or otherwise stop execution of the rest of the function. In Example 16-15, if the user ID assertion fails, it still attempts to make the PUT request to update the user. This likely results in a 404 error because `null` is in the URL.

16.11 Examining an Object's Properties

Problem

You want to inspect the properties of an object, including deeply nested ones and the prototype chain.

Solution

Use `console.dir` to log the object.

Example 16-16 shows how to use `console.dir` to inspect the `console` object itself.

Example 16-16. Using `console.dir`

```
console.dir(console);
```

Figure 16-11 shows the expandable tree structure that is logged to the console. Each function and property in the object is expandable. It also includes the prototype chain, which can be expanded and inspected as well.

```
▼ console ⓘ
  ▶ assert: ƒ assert()
  ▶ clear: ƒ clear()
  ▶ context: ƒ context()
  ▶ count: ƒ count()
  ▶ countReset: ƒ countReset()
  ▶ createTask: ƒ createTask()
  ▶ debug: ƒ debug()
  ▶ dir: ƒ dir()
  ▶ dirxml: ƒ dirxml()
  ▶ error: ƒ error()
  ▶ group: ƒ group()
  ▶ groupCollapsed: ƒ groupCollapsed()
  ▶ groupEnd: ƒ groupEnd()
  ▶ info: ƒ info()
  ▶ log: ƒ log()
  ▶ memory: MemoryInfo {totalJSHeapSize: 10000000, usedJSHeapSize: 10000000, jsHeapSizeLimit: 3760000000}
  ▶ profile: ƒ profile()
  ▶ profileEnd: ƒ profileEnd()
  ▶ table: ƒ table()
  ▶ time: ƒ time()
  ▶ timeEnd: ƒ timeEnd()
  ▶ timeLog: ƒ timeLog()
  ▶ timeStamp: ƒ timeStamp()
  ▶ trace: ƒ trace()
  ▶ warn: ƒ warn(...args)
    Symbol(Symbol.toStringTag): "console"
  ▶ [[Prototype]]: Object
```

Figure 16-11. Using `console.dir` on the console object (shown in Chrome)

Discussion

On some browser versions, `console.log` also presents an interactive structure to inspect an object. While this behavior is browser dependent, `console.dir` always inspects the object, as shown in Figure 16-11.

For more information, you can look at the official console specification (*https:// oreil.ly/osZhg*).

CHAPTER 17

CSS

17.0 Introduction

In the modern browser environment, CSS not only lets you write style rules but also has a set of APIs you can use to further enhance your application.

The CSS Object Model (CSSOM) allows you to set inline styles programmatically from JavaScript code. Not only that, but you can even change the values of CSS variables at runtime.

In Chapter 8, you saw an example of using `window.matchMedia` to programmatically check a media query to see if it matches on the current page.

This chapter has some helpful recipes that use some of these CSS-related APIs. At the time of writing, some of these APIs do not have good browser support. Always check browser compatibility before using them.

17.1 Highlighting Text Ranges

Problem

You want to apply a highlight effect to a range of text in the document.

Solution

Create a `Range` object around the desired text, then use the CSS Custom Highlight API to apply the highlighting styles to that range.

The first step is to create a `Range` object. This object represents a region of text within the document. Example 17-1 shows a general purpose utility function to create a range given a text node and the text to highlight.

Example 17-1. Creating a Range

```
/**
 * Given a text node and a substring to highlight, creates a Range object covering
 * the desired text.
 */
function getRange(textNode, textToHighlight) {
  const startOffset = textNode.textContent.indexOf(textToHighlight);
  const endOffset = startOffset + textToHighlight.length;

  // Create a Range for the text to highlight.
  const range = new Range();
  range.setStart(textNode, startOffset);
  range.setEnd(textNode, endOffset);

  return range;
}
```

This API may not be supported by all browsers yet. See CanIUse (*https://oreil.ly/wDJWH*) for the latest compatibility data.

Suppose you have the HTML element shown in Example 17-2.

Example 17-2. Some HTML markup

```
<p id="text">
  This is some text. We're using the CSS Custom Highlight API to highlight some of
  the text.
</p>
```

If you wanted to highlight the text "highlight some of the text," you can use the getRange helper to create a Range around that text (see Example 17-3).

Example 17-3. Using the getRange helper

```
const node = document.querySelector('#text');
const range = getRange(node.firstChild, 'highlight some of the text');
```

Now that you have the range, you need to register a new highlight with the browser's highlight registry. Do this by creating a new Highlight object with the range, and then pass that Highlight to the CSS.highlights.set function (see Example 17-4).

Example 17-4. Registering the highlight

```
const highlight = new Highlight(range);
CSS.highlights.set('highlight-range', highlight);
```

This registers the highlight, but by default this has no visual effect. Next, you need to create some CSS styles that you'd like to apply to the highlight. This is done by using the ::highlight pseudo-element. You use this pseudo-element combined with the key you registered the Highlight under in Example 17-4 (see Example 17-5).

Example 17-5. Styling the highlight

```
::highlight(highlight-range) {
  background-color: #fef3c7;
}
```

With this style applied, the text inside the range is now highlighted with a light amber color.

Discussion

You can also highlight content by using the <mark> element. Example 17-6 shows how to highlight some text with <mark>.

Example 17-6. Highlighting using the mark element

```
<p id="text">
  This is some text. We're using the mark element to
  <mark>highlight some of the text</mark>.
</p>
```

This has the same visual effect as using the CSS Custom Highlight API, but the key difference is that using <mark> involves inserting a new element into the DOM. This can be tricky depending on where you are adding the new element.

For example, if the text you want to highlight spans multiple elements, it may not be possible to do this with a <mark> element and still be valid HTML. Consider the HTML in Example 17-7.

Example 17-7. Some markup to highlight

```
<p>
  This is a paragraph, which is being highlighted.
</p>
```

```
<p>
  The highlight extends to this paragraph. This is not highlighted.
</p>
```

If you want to highlight "which is being highlighted. The highlight extends to this paragraph," you can't do this with a single <mark> element (see Example 17-8).

Example 17-8. Invalid HTML

```
<p>
  This is a paragraph, <mark>which is being highlighted.
</p>

<p>
  The highlight extends to this paragraph</mark>. This is not highlighted.
</p>
```

This is not valid HTML. The solution would be to use two separate <mark> elements, but then it's not a single continuous highlighted region.

Using the CSS Custom Highlight API makes such highlighting possible by creating a range that spans multiple tags and applying the highlight effect.

17.2 Preventing a Flash of Unstyled Text

Problem

You want to avoid the flash of unstyled text when using web fonts.

Solution

Use the CSS Font Loading API to explicitly load the font faces you want to use in your application, and delay rendering any text until the fonts have been loaded.

To load a font with this API, you first create a FontFace object containing data about the font face you want to load. Example 17-9 uses the Roboto font.

Example 17-9. Creating the Roboto font face

```
const roboto = new FontFace(
  'Roboto',
  'url(https://fonts.gstatic.com/s/roboto/v30/KFOmCnqEu92Fr1Mu72xKKTU1Kvnz.woff2)', {
    style: 'normal',
    weight: 400
  });
```

The document has a global `fonts` property, which is a `FontFaceSet`, containing all of the font faces used in the document. In order to use this font face, you need to add it to the `FontFaceSet` (see Example 17-10).

Example 17-10. Adding Roboto to the global `FontFaceSet`

```
document.fonts.add(roboto);
```

So far, you've only defined the font. Nothing has been loaded yet. You can start the loading process by calling `load` on the `FontFace` object (see Example 17-11). This returns a `Promise` that is resolved once the font is loaded.

Example 17-11. Waiting for the font to be loaded

```
roboto.load()
  .then(() => {
    // Font has been loaded and is ready for use.
  });
```

To prevent the flash of unstyled text, you'll need to hide the text that uses this font until it has finished loading. If your app shows an initial loading animation, for example, you could continue the animation until the necessary fonts are loaded, then remove the loader and start rendering the app.

If your app is using multiple fonts, you can wait for the `document.fonts.ready` `Promise`. This `Promise` is resolved once all fonts are loaded and ready.

Discussion

When using web fonts with CSS, fonts are declared with a `@font-face` rule, which contains the URL of the font file to download. If text is rendered before the font has finished loading, a fallback system font is used. Once the font is ready, the text is re-rendered with the correct font. This can cause undesirable effects such as layout shifts if the font metrics are different.

The downside of using `@font-face` is that you have no way of knowing when the font has been loaded and is ready for use. By using the CSS Font Loading API, you can get better control over your font loading and know exactly when it's safe to start using a given font to render text.

If there is an error while loading the font—for example, maybe you mistyped the font URL—the `Promise` returned by the font's `load` method rejects with the error.

17.3 Animating DOM Transitions

Problem

You want to show an animated transition when removing or adding elements to the DOM.

Solution

Use the View Transitions API to provide an animated transition between the two states.

 This API may not be supported by all browsers yet. See CanIUse (*https://oreil.ly/I8RFN*) for the latest compatibility data.

This API is used to apply a transition effect between two DOM states. To start a view transition, call the `document.startViewTransition` function. This function takes a callback function as its argument. You need to perform your DOM changes within this callback function.

In Example 17-12, imagine you have a single-page app. Each view of the app is a top-level HTML element with a unique ID. To route between views, you can remove the current view and add the new one.

Example 17-12. A simple view transition

```
function showAboutPage() {
  document.startViewTransition(() => {
    document.querySelector('#home-page').style.display = 'none';
    document.querySelector('#about-page').style.display = 'block';
  });
}
```

This applies a basic cross-fade transition effect between the two views.

If you want to adjust the speed of the cross-fade transition, you can do so with a bit of CSS, as shown in Example 17-13.

Example 17-13. Slowing down the transition

```
::view-transition-old(root),
::view-transition-new(root) {
```

```
    animation-duration: 2s;
}
```

Discussion

The view transition effect works by effectively taking a screenshot of the current DOM state. Once the DOM changes inside the callback are made, another screenshot is taken. The browser creates some pseudo-elements on the page and applies an animated transition between them.

The pseudo-elements created are:

`::view-transition`
:   A top-level overlay containing all view transitions

`::view-transition-group(<name>)`
:   An individual view transition

`::view-transition-image-pair(<name>)`
:   Contains the two images being transitioned

`::view-transition-old(<name>)`
:   Image of the old DOM state

`::view-transition-new(<name>)`
:   Image of the new DOM state

Some of these pseudo-elements take a `name` argument. This can be one of the following:

`*`
:   Matches all view transition groups

`root`
:   Matches the `root` transition group, which is the default name if no custom name is given.

A custom identifier
:   You can specify the custom identifier by setting the `view-transition-name` property on the element to be transitioned.

You can use CSS selectors to target these pseudo-elements and apply different animations. You can do this by creating a `@keyframes` rule for the animation and applying that animation to the `::view-transition-old` or `::view-transition-new` pseudo-elements.

17.4 Modifying Stylesheets at Runtime

Problem

You want to dynamically add a CSS rule to a stylesheet on the page.

Solution

Use the `insertRule` method of `CSSStyleSheet` to add the desired rule (see Example 17-14).

Example 17-14. Adding a CSS rule

```
const [stylesheet] = document.styleSheets;
stylesheet.insertRule(`
  .some-selector {
    background-color: red;
  }
`);
```

Discussion

You might want to do this if you have new HTML content that is dynamically added to the page, such as in a single-page application. You can dynamically add the style rules when the new content is added.

17.5 Conditionally Setting a CSS Class

Problem

You want to apply a CSS class to an element only if a certain condition is met.

Solution

Use the `toggle` method of the element's `classList` (see Example 17-15).

Example 17-15. Toggling a class conditionally

```
// Assume isExpanded is a variable with the current expanded
// state
element.classList.toggle('expanded', isExpanded);
```

Discussion

If you call `toggle` without the second argument, it adds the class name if it's not currently set, or removes it if it's already set.

In addition to `toggle`, you can use `add` and `remove` to manipulate the class list by adding and removing the given class name. If you call `add` when the class name is already set, it has no effect. Similarly, if you call `remove` when the class name isn't set, it also has no effect.

17.6 Matching Media Queries

Problem

You want to check if a certain media query is satisfied using JavaScript. For example, you might want to use the `prefers-color-scheme` media query to determine if a user's operating system is set to a dark theme.

Solution

Use `window.matchMedia` to evaluate the media query or listen for changes (see Example 17-16).

Example 17-16. Checking for a dark color scheme

```
const isDarkTheme = window.matchMedia('(prefers-color-scheme: dark)').matches;
```

Discussion

`window.matchMedia` returns a `MediaQueryList` object that not only has the `matches` property but also lets you listen for the `change` event. This event fires if the result of the media query changes.

For example, if the user's operating system color theme setting changes while your app is open, the `change` event fires for the `prefers-color-scheme` query. You can then check for the new match state (see Example 17-17).

Example 17-17. Listening for media query changes

```
const query = window.matchMedia('(prefers-color-scheme: dark)');
query.addEventListener('change', () => {
  if (query.matches) {
    // switch to dark mode
  } else {
    // switch to light mode
```

```
  }
});
```

17.7 Getting an Element's Computed Style

Problem

You want to find a particular CSS style for an element that comes from a stylesheet (not an inline style).

Solution

Use `window.getComputedStyle` to calculate the final styles for the element.

Use getComputedStyle Sparingly

When you call `getComputedStyle`, it forces the browser to recalculate styles and layout, which can be a performance bottleneck.

Consider the HTML element in Example 17-18 with some styling applied.

Example 17-18. Some HTML with style

```
<style>
  #content {
    background-color: blue;
  }

  .container {
    background-color: red;
    color: white;
  }
</style>

<div id="content" class="container">What color am I?</div>
```

To determine the styles that are applied to the element, pass the element to win dow.getComputedStyle (see Example 17-19).

Example 17-19. Getting the computed style

```
const content = document.querySelector('#content');
const styles = window.getComputedStyle(content);
console.log(styles.backgroundColor);
```

Because the ID selector has a higher specificity than the class selector, it wins the conflict and `styles.backgroundColor` is blue. On some browsers, it may not be the string "blue" but rather a color expression such as `rgb(0, 0, 255)`.

Discussion

An element's `style` property only works for *inline styles*. Consider Example 17-20.

Example 17-20. An element with inline styles

```
<style>
  #content {
    background-color: blue;
  }
</style>

<div id="content" style="color: white;">Content</div>
```

This example specifies the `color` property as an inline style, so you can access this by referencing the `style` property. However, the background color comes from a stylesheet and won't be found this way (see Example 17-21).

Example 17-21. Checking inline styles

```
const content = document.querySelector('#content');
console.log(content.style.backgroundColor); // empty string
console.log(content.style.color); // 'white'
```

Since `getComputedStyle` calculates the final style of the element, it contains both stylesheet styles and inline styles (see Example 17-22).

Example 17-22. Checking computed styles

```
const content = document.querySelector('#content');
const styles = window.getComputedStyle(content);
console.log(styles.backgroundColor); // 'rgb(0, 0, 255)'
console.log(styles.color); // 'rgb(255, 255, 255)'
```

CHAPTER 18

Media

18.0 Introduction

Modern browsers have rich APIs for working with video and audio streams. The WebRTC API supports creating these streams from devices such as cameras.

A video stream can be played live inside of a <video> element, and from there you can capture a frame of the video to save as an image or upload to an API. A <video> element can also be used to play back video that was recorded from a stream.

Before these APIs were available, you would have needed browser plug-ins to access the user's camera. Today, you can use the Media Capture and Streams API to start reading data from the camera and microphone with just a small amount of code.

18.1 Recording the Screen

Problem

You want to capture a video of the user's screen.

Solution

Use the Screen Capture API to capture a video of the screen, then set it as the source of a <video> element (see Example 18-1).

Example 18-1. Capturing a video of the screen

```
async function captureScreen() {
  const stream = await navigator.mediaDevices.getDisplayMedia();
  const mediaRecorder = new MediaRecorder(stream, {
```

```
    mimeType: 'video/webm'
  });

  mediaRecorder.addEventListener('dataavailable', event => {
    const blob = new Blob([event.data], {
      type: 'video/webm',
    });

    const url = URL.createObjectURL(blob);
    video.src = url;
  });

  mediaRecorder.start();
}
```

 The screen contents are not streamed live to the `<video>` element. Rather, the screen share is captured into memory. Once you've finished capturing the screen, the recorded video will play in the `<video>` element.

There's a lot going on here. First, call `navigator.mediaDevices.getDisplayMedia()` to initiate a screen capture. Depending on the browser and operating system, you will get some sort of prompt about screen recording (see Figure 18-1).

Figure 18-1. Screen recording prompt from Chrome on macOS

This function returns a `Promise` that resolves to a `MediaStream` of the user's screen. Once this `Promise` resolves, the screen is being recorded, but the data isn't going anywhere yet.

To stop recording, click the browser-provided button to stop sharing or call `mediaRecorder.stop()`. This will trigger the `dataavailable` event.

Next, the event handler creates a `Blob` containing the captured video data and creates an object URL. You can then set the video's `src` attribute to this object URL.

Once this is done, the screen recording will start playing in the browser.

Discussion

This example uses the `video/webm` MIME type, which has good browser support. WebM is an open audio and video file format that supports multiple codecs.

If the user does not give permission for screen recording, the `Promise` returned by `getDisplayMedia` will be rejected with an error.

This example shows how to play back the screen recording in a `<video>` element, but there are other things you can do once you have the `Blob` and object URL.

For example, you could send the `Blob` to a server using the Fetch API (see Example 18-2).

Example 18-2. Uploading the captured screen recording

```
const form = new FormData();
// Here, "blob" is the Blob created in the captureScreen method.
formData.append('file', blob);

fetch('/api/video/upload', {
  method: 'POST',
  body: formData
});
```

You could also trigger the browser to download the captured video (see Example 18-3).

Example 18-3. Triggering a download with a hidden link

```
const link = document.createElement('a');

// Here, "url" is the object URL created in the captureScreen method.
link.href = url;
link.textContent = 'Download';
```

```
link.download = 'screen-recording.webm';
link.click();
```

18.2 Capturing an Image from the User's Camera

Problem

You want to activate the user's camera and take a photo.

Solution

Use `navigator.mediaDevices.getUserMedia` to get video from the camera.

First, you'll need to create a few elements, as shown in Example 18-4.

Example 18-4. The markup for capturing an image from the camera

```
<style>
  #canvas {
    display: none;
  }

  #photo {
    width: 640px;
    height: 480px;
  }
</style>

<canvas id="canvas"></canvas>
<img id="photo">
<video id="preview">
```

The canvas is hidden because it's an intermediate step before producing an image.

The general approach is as follows:

1. Send the video stream to the <video> element to show a live preview from the camera.

2. When you want to capture a photo, draw the current video frame on the canvas.

3. Create a data URL from the canvas to generate a JPEG image, and set it in the <img> element.

First, open the video stream and attach it to the <video> element (see Example 18-5).

Example 18-5. Getting the video stream

```
const preview = document.querySelector('#preview');

async function startCamera() {
  const stream = await navigator.mediaDevices.getUserMedia(
    {
      video: true,
      audio: false
    }
  );
  preview.srcObject = stream;
  preview.play();
}
```

Later, capture the image in response to a button click or other event (see Example 18-6).

Example 18-6. Capturing the image

```
// This is the <video> element.
const preview = document.querySelector('#preview');

const photo = document.querySelector('#photo');
const canvas = document.querySelector('#canvas');

function captureImage() {
  // Resize the canvas based on the device pixel density.
  // This helps prevent a blurred or pixellated image.
  canvas.width = canvas.width * window.devicePixelRatio;
  canvas.height = canvas.height * window.devicePixelRatio;

  // Get the 2D context from the canvas and draw the current video frame.
  const context = canvas.getContext('2d');
  context.drawImage(preview, 0, 0, canvas.width, canvas.height);

  // Create a JPEG data URL and set it as the image source.
  const dataUrl = canvas.toDataURL('image/jpeg');
  photo.src = dataUrl;
}
```

Discussion

As you might expect, reading from the camera raises privacy concerns. As such, opening the user's camera for the first time will trigger a permission request in the browser that the user must accept to grant access. If this request is denied, the Promise returned by navigator.mediaDevices.getUserMedia will be rejected with an error.

18.3 Capturing a Video from the User's Camera

Problem

You want to record a video from the user's camera and play it back in the browser.

Solution

This solution has several steps:

1. Use `getUserMedia` to open a stream from the camera.
2. Use a `<video>` element to show a preview of the video.
3. Use a `MediaRecorder` to record the video.
4. Play back the recorded video in the `<video>` element.

For this recipe, you need the `<video>` element and buttons to start and stop recording (see Example 18-7).

Example 18-7. Setting up the video element

```
<video id="preview" muted></video>
<button id="record-button">Record</button>
<button id="stop-record-button">Stop Recording</button>
```

Next, open the video stream and set the `<video>` element to preview it (see Example 18-8).

Example 18-8. Opening the audio and video stream

```
const preview = document.querySelector('#preview');

const stream = await navigator.mediaDevices.getUserMedia({
  video: true,
  audio: true
});
preview.srcObject = stream;
preview.play();
```

Once the stream is open, the next step is to set up the `MediaRecorder` (see Example 18-9).

Example 18-9. Setting up the `MediaRecorder`

```
mediaRecorder = new MediaRecorder(stream, {
  mimeType: 'video/webm'
```

```
});

mediaRecorder.addEventListener('dataavailable', event => {
  const blob = new Blob([event.data], {
    type: 'video/webm',
  });

  const url = URL.createObjectURL(blob);

  // Clear the "muted" flag so that the playback will
  // include audio.
  preview.muted = false;

  // Reset the source of the video element to the object
  // URL just created.
  preview.srcObject = null;
  preview.src = url;

  // Start playing the recording immediately.
  preview.autoplay = true;
  preview.loop = true;
  preview.controls = true;
});
```

The last step is to wire up the buttons to start and stop the MediaRecorder (see Example 18-10).

Example 18-10. Adding button event handlers

```
document.querySelector('#record-button').addEventListener('click', () => {
  mediaRecorder.start();
});

document.querySelector('#stop-record-button').addEventListener('click', () => {
  mediaRecorder.stop();
});
```

Discussion

You might have noticed the video element initially had the muted attribute set on it. The media stream you open will have both video and audio. You want to preview the video, but you probably don't want to preview the audio—this would cause whatever audio is recorded to immediately play back on the speakers, which could affect the recording or even cause microphone feedback. To prevent this, you can set the muted attribute on the <video> element.

Later, when it's time to play back what you recorded, you are clearing the muted flag so that the recorded audio will play as well.

18.4 Determining the System Media Capabilities

Problem

You want to know if a particular media type is supported by the browser.

Solution

Use the Media Capabilities API to query the browser for the given media type. The result will tell you if that media type is supported or not (see Example 18-11).

Example 18-11. Checking media capabilities

```
navigator.mediaCapabilities.decodingInfo({
  type: 'file',
  audio: {
    contentType: 'audio/mp3'
  }
}).then(result => {
  if (result.supported) {
    // mp3 audio is supported!
  }
});

navigator.mediaCapabilities.decodingInfo({
  type: 'file',
  audio: {
    contentType: 'audio/webm;codecs=opus'
  }
}).then(result => {
  if (result.supported) {
    // WebM audio is supported with the opus codec.
  }
});
```

Discussion

Example 18-11 shows some examples of checking for audio codec support. The Media Capabilities API also lets you check for specific video format support. You can query not only by codec, but also by other attributes such as frame rate, bitrate, width, and height (see Example 18-12).

Example 18-12. Checking for a supported video format

```
navigator.mediaCapabilities.decodingInfo({
  type: 'file',
  video: {
    contentType: 'video/webm;codecs=vp8',
```

```
      bitrate: 4000000, // 4 MB
      framerate: 30,
      width: 1920,
      height: 1080
    }
}).then(result => {
  if (result.supported) {
    // This WebM configuration is supported.
  }
});
```

18.5 Applying Video Filters

Problem

You want to apply a filter effect to a video stream.

Solution

Render the video stream to a `<canvas>`, and apply a CSS filter to the canvas.

You'll set the video stream as the source of a `<video>` element, as in Recipe 18.2. However, in this case you'll hide the `<video>` element as it's just an intermediate step.

Then, based on your desired frame rate, render each frame of the video to a `<canvas>` element. From there, you can apply CSS filters.

First, the markup (see Example 18-13).

Example 18-13. Markup for the video filter example

```
<canvas id="canvas"></canvas>
<video id="preview" style="display: none;"></video>
```

Then, open the media stream and set it in the `<video>` element (see Example 18-14).

Example 18-14. Setting up the video stream

```
async function startCamera() {
  const stream = await navigator.mediaDevices.getUserMedia({
    video: true,
    audio: false
  });

  // Hook up the video element to the stream.
  preview.srcObject = stream;
  preview.play();

  // Resize the canvas based on the device pixel density.
```

```
  // This helps prevent a blurred or pixelated image.
  canvas.width = canvas.width * window.devicePixelRatio;
  canvas.height = canvas.height * window.devicePixelRatio;
  const context = canvas.getContext('2d');

  // Target frame rate of 30 FPS—draw each frame to the canvas.
  setInterval(() => {
    context.drawImage(preview, 0, 0, canvas.width, canvas.height);
  }, 30 / 1000);
}
```

Now, you can apply a CSS filter to the <canvas> element (see Example 18-15).

Example 18-15. Applying a filter

```
#canvas {
  filter: hue-rotate(90deg);
}
```

Discussion

Every 0.03 seconds, the current frame of the video will be drawn to the canvas. This is effectively a preview of the media stream, using the <video> element as an intermediate. This is because there's currently no way to "draw" a video from a media stream directly to a <canvas> element.

In addition to setting the filters with CSS, you can also set them using the filter property of the canvas 2D context.

CHAPTER 19

Closing Thoughts

19.0 Introduction

I hope you've found the recipes and APIs covered in this book to be useful and interesting. Hopefully you've been able to apply what you've learned in this book to level up your JavaScript applications.

19.1 In Defense of Third-Party Libraries

One of the main themes of this book is the fact that you can do so much without needing third-party libraries. This is true, but don't feel like you have to avoid third-party libraries at all costs. Sometimes using the built-in browser APIs saves you from needing a dependency, but you might have to write extra "glue" code to adapt it to what you're trying to accomplish.

Some browser APIs can be awkward to work with. Take the IndexedDB API, for example. It's a powerful data persistence and access layer, but its API is callback based and can be painful to work with. There are libraries available that wrap IndexedDB and provide a simpler—or, in some cases, more powerful—API. For example, Dexie.js wraps IndexedDB with a `Promise`-based API.

In the end, everything is a trade-off. If you have room to spare in your JavaScript bundle to provide an easier developer experience, it's probably worth it.

19.2 Detect Features, Not Browser Versions

If you need to check if the user is running a browser that supports the API you want to use, you might think to look at the user agent string and figure out which browser version the user has. Try to avoid this. It is notoriously unreliable, plus it's trivial to spoof the user agent string to masquerade as another browser.

Instead, detect if a particular feature is available. For example, if you wanted to check if the browser supports IndexedDB, just check for the presence of the `indexedDB` property in the `window` object (see Example 19-1).

Example 19-1. Checking for IndexedDB support

```
if ('indexedDB' in window) {
  // IndexedDB is supported!
}
```

19.3 Polyfills

If you need to support older browsers, you may be able to still use some of these APIs with a polyfill. This is a third-party JavaScript library that adds the missing functionality. These polyfills may not be as performant as the built-in APIs, but they allow you to use newer APIs in browsers that otherwise wouldn't support them.

Some APIs can't be polyfilled, of course, because they rely on integration with native device capabilities like the accelerometer or geolocation. If the browser has no way to communicate with these system services, no amount of third-party code can bridge that gap.

19.4 Looking Ahead to the Future

There are even more exciting APIs on the horizon that will further expand what you can do in browser-based apps without needing plug-ins or third-party libraries. To close out the book, this section briefly looks at some upcoming experimental APIs that will enrich browser apps even more in the near future.

Web Bluetooth API

Soon you'll be able to interact with Bluetooth devices natively in the browser using the Web Bluetooth API. It provides a `Promise`-based interface for discovering and reading information about connected Bluetooth devices. You can read data such as battery level, or listen for notifications from devices.

This works by interacting with the device's GATT (Generic Attribute) Profile, which defines supported services and characteristics for a Bluetooth device. This keeps the API generic, allowing it the flexibility to work with any kind of device that supports GATT.

Web NFC API

Near-field communication (NFC) allows devices to exchange information when they are in close proximity to one another. The Web NFC API will allow devices to exchange messages and information with NFC hardware.

This API provides the ability to exchange messages using the NFC Data Exchange Format (NDEF). This is a standardized format published by the NFC Forum.

EyeDropper API

The EyeDropper API will allow you to select a color from pixels on the screen via an eye dropper tool. This tool will work both inside and outside the browser window, allowing you to pick a color from anywhere on the screen.

You can construct an eye dropper by calling the `EyeDropper` constructor. The `Eye Dropper` provides an `open` method that shows an eye dropper interface on the screen, and returns a `Promise`. Once you select a pixel with the eye dropper, the `Promise` resolves with the color of the selected pixel.

Barcode Detection API

This API will give your applications the ability to read barcodes and QR codes. It supports many types of standard barcode types. This will be a versatile API that can read barcodes from many different image sources: image and video elements, Blobs, canvas elements, and more.

Barcodes are detected by passing image data to a `BarcodeDetector`'s `detect` method. This returns a `Promise` that resolves to data about any detected barcodes and their values.

Cookie Store API

The current mechanism for working with cookies in the browser is not very convenient. The `document.cookie` property is a single string that contains key/value pair mappings of cookie names and values for the current site.

The upcoming Cookie Store API provides an asynchronous, more robust interface for accessing cookie information. You can look up the details of a single cookie with the `CookieStore.get` method, which returns a `Promise` that resolves to information about the cookie with the given name.

It also lets you listen to `change` events, which are fired whenever cookie data changes.

Payment APIs

The Payment Request API provides a way for a website to initiate a payment in the browser. You can then use the Payment Handler API to process the payment without having to redirect to another website.

This will let you provide a more consistent experience when using an external payment processor.

Finding What's Next

The web is always changing. If you want to get a peek at what other web browser APIs are coming, some good resources are:

- MDN Web Docs (*https://oreil.ly/PqBPh*) has a Web APIs page (*https://oreil.ly/YTWkO*) that shows an overview of current and upcoming or experimental APIs.

- The W3C standards and drafts page (*https://oreil.ly/Xu47E*) contains a searchable directory of standards and draft specifications at all levels of development.

Index

uploading file data with the Fetch API, 48
price ranges, formatting, 152
profile card, web components for, 170-172
Promises
    asynchronous APIs and, 2
    chaining, 6-7
    creating a Promise helper for speech recognition, 127-128
    event API wrapping, 12-13
    events versus, 2
    handling error case, 3
    Image element and, 4
    parallel, 8-9
    using with IndexedDB API, 70-72
    working with, 2-3
    wrapping IntersectionObserver with, 76-77
push notifications, 195

Q

QR codes, 259
query parameters, for URLs
    adding, 33-35
    reading, 36
    removing, 36
querying, with IndexedDB, 64-66
queryPermission function, 141-142

R

registering custom elements, 162
relative URLs, resolving, 30-31
remote events, listening for, 50-51
rendering performance, profiling, 215-216
replacer function, 21
requestAnimationFrame
    animating elements with, 9-12
    scheduling updates with, 18
requests
    finding timings for specific resource requests, 214
    in IndexedDB, 57
ResizeObserver, 74, 81
resolving relative URLs, 30-31
Resource Timing API, 211
resources
    finding slowest, 213
    finding timings for, 214
    performance measurement, 213
reverse geocoding, 202
reviver function, 22

RFC 3986 (Uniform Resource Identifier: Generic Syntax), 29
"ripple" animation, 107-109
rounding, of decimal places, 152
routers
    client-side, 37-39
    matching to patterns, 41
routing
    adding query parameters for URLs, 33-35
    creating a simple client-side router, 37-39
    removing query parameters for URLs, 32-33
runtime, modifying stylesheets at, 242

S

screen, capturing video of, 247-249
scroll progress indicator, 115-116
scroll-linked animation, 116
scrolling, infinite, 83
ScrollTimeline, 116
sentences, counting, 155-157
server-sent events (SSEs), 50-51
setCustomValidity method, 97-98
shadow DOM, 163, 168-169
simple objects, persisting to local storage, 18-20
<slot> element, 163
    for customizable confirmation dialogs, 185-187
    for disclosure web component, 173-176
    for profile card, 170-172
    for profile card components, 170-172
specifications and standards, sources for, xi
speech recognition, 123
    creating a Promise helper, 127-128
    language processing versus, 124
speech synthesis, 124, 130
    customizing parameters, 131
    getting available voices, 129
Speech Synthesis Markup Language (SSML), 125
SpeechRecognition interface, 125-127
SSEs (server-sent events), 50-51
stack traces, logging, 230
storage (see Web Storage API)
Storage interface, 15
string data, persisting to local storage, 18
string values, cursors for finding, 67-68
styled button component, 176-178
stylesheets

About the Author

Joe Attardi has more than 20 years of frontend software development experience and has built many browser-based applications. He's also built rich frontend experiences for Nortel, Dell, Constant Contact, Salesforce, and Synopsys, and he specializes in JavaScript and TypeScript development.

Colophon

The animal on the cover of *Web API Cookbook* is a golden-headed quetzal (*Pharomachrus auriceps*). These birds live in humid forests from Panama to Bolivia.

The word *quetzal* comes from *quetzalli*, which means "long green plume" in the Aztec language Nahuatl. Quetzals are known for their iridescent green plumage and red belly. The golden-headed quetzal is named for its brilliant golden head. Females have more brown feathers than the males. The weigh from 154 to 182 grams and are 33–36 centimeters long, with the males being larger.

Quetzals are solitary birds until breeding season, when males and females pair and build a nest together in a decaying tree trunk. Females lay 1–2 pale blue eggs and then both birds brood and share responsibility for feeding the chicks. The birds eat mostly fruit, and they are therefore important to the dispersal of fruit seeds in their habitat.

The golden-headed quetzal is common in its range and has an IUCN status as a species of least concern. Many of the animals on O'Reilly covers are endangered; all of them are important to the world.

The cover illustration is by Karen Montgomery, based on an antique line engraving from *Routledge's Picture Natural History*. The series design is by Edie Freedman, Ellie Volckhausen, and Karen Montgomery. The cover fonts are Gilroy Semibold and Guardian Sans. The text font is Adobe Minion Pro; the heading font is Adobe Myriad Condensed; and the code font is Dalton Maag's Ubuntu Mono.

O'REILLY®

Learn from experts.
Become one yourself.

Books | Live online courses
Instant answers | Virtual events
Videos | Interactive learning

Get started at oreilly.com.

Printed in the USA
CPSIA information can be obtained
at www.ICGtesting.com
JSHW050026090724
66058JS00007B/94